Unsafe In Human Hands

The human stories behind gun ownership and violence in America.

By

Christopher Linley Johnson

The Linley Company
New York

Dedication

I dedicate this book to all those brave souls who try to save the rest of us from ourselves, especially the Violence Interrupters at Cure Violence who risk personal danger to de-escalate potentially violent situations before they result in bloodshed. One hundred percent of the author's proceeds from this book will be donated to Cure Violence, Chicago, IL.

TABLE OF CONTENTS

Acknowledgements

The best qualities of this book can be attributed to my dear friend Joy Carol, a successful author in her own right, who served as my editor and coach.   Joy is also a spiritual director and workshop and retreat leader and a beloved figure at my church - the Cathedral of St. John the Divine. Joy's own books make use of personal stories as a means of approaching difficult subjects and her particular format inspired mine. In helping me to finish my own book, I cannot thank her enough for her time and enthusiasm.

To the many persons who told me their stories, especially Edwin Garcia, I am grateful for your passion and openness. I could not have written this book without the support and input from true friends. I regret that every one of you could not be included in this book. Each of your stories deserves a book of your own. Maybe that will be my next opus.

Introduction

The events of December 14, 2012 at Sandy Hook Elementary shocked me from a state of complacency. Along with so many Americans, this was a watershed moment for me that focused attention on the problem of violence in our country in a way it never had done before. And yet, on a personal level, I didn't know what to do – only that I wanted to do something.

I suspected that the study of violence and the role of guns were going to be complex. In my attempt to better understand the dimensions of the problem, I began reading all the quality research on the subject I could find. What started as a personal journey of inquiry ultimately turned into this book. It highlights the conclusions I've come to during this journey, and in the end, I hope it helps contribute positively to our public debate.

My worry is that the ensuing conversation will be one about guns, which are only things, when it should remain about people. Guns are only the gasoline poured onto a fire, volatile to be sure, but only part of the story. By contrast, people, in all their infinite diversity and complexity, should remain our spiritual and moral priority. And therefore the focus of this debate.

Often it takes a particular human element to make a story resonate with the public. Statistics never do it. For those of us old enough to remember the Vietnam War, the photos in *Life Magazine* of the 200 Americans who had died that week or the image of a Buddhist monk named Thich Quang Duc who, in order to protest, set himself on fire in a busy Saigon intersection, all combined to change America's mindset on that war. It made it personal. The five and six year olds in Newtown, CT have certainly done the same, making this story resonate with us now.

Surely, in any subject of national importance, saving lives first should be our most worthy endeavor. Few of us would fail to rescue a child from harm if we saw them running out into a busy street. But on a national scale, it is harder to find our role in such a matter. Who are we to each other and how does that play to this issue? What is our obligation to one another in society? Are we our brother's keeper?

The victims of violent deaths are often our most vulnerable citizens; those with suicidal tendencies and young adults. Young people are doubly at-risk; those aged 15-24 are most likely to experience a serious violent crime and also are the ones most likely to commit one. Therefore, at the worst moment in someone's life, when they are, for whatever reason, making the worst decisions they could possibly ever make, how does a gun end up in their hands? And who is responsible? What is the broader social responsibility as well as the cost to society on these issues? With the highest cost in terms of lost youth, both those who die and those who spend the rest of their lives incarcerated, it is incumbent upon us adults to consider these matters seriously. Aren't we supposed to be the ones to shepherd these youth through troubled waters into positive adulthood? Do we cast them to the wolves?

Part of the difficulty in discussing these issues is a gap in our perceptions of the problem. There are a few mistaken myths which impede our ability to see things clearly. For example, too many of the recent mass shootings – horrible as they have been - have mistakenly focused the debate on the lone "madman" – the maladjusted person someone should have identified earlier on. In fact, the bulk of gun shootings are not like that. It is one point we need to clarify if we are to get this fixed.

Another involves the concept of the law-abiding-gun-owner. The truth is that any good person who under normal circumstances might never have harmed another soul, could in a moment of extreme rage make a very bad choice. Add a fire arm to that scenario, and you have permanent, unfixable damage. To say gun owners fall into only two categories; law abiding citizens and the few mentally unstable outcasts, is to both over simplify and to dangerously get it wrong. Studies show that individuals in possession of a gun are 4.46 times more likely to be shot in an assault than those not in possession (American Public Health Associations 2009 study "Investigating the Link Between Gun Possession and Gun Assault"). The truth? Gun possession increases risk to the gun holder and those around him. Gasoline on a fire.

In later chapters, we will review dramatic demographic shifts which are causing the evolution of two different Americas. These have profound effects on all our political and social viewpoints. In particular, the tipping point – the move toward urbanization – has the greatest impact on one's attitude toward gun ownership and the threat of violence. Clarity about these demographics will surely increase our mutual understanding and further help us to plan strategies for change.

Any gun discussion must include consideration of the Constitution and the Second Amendment. It would be impossible in any society to casually throw out our mutual social compact without serious consideration to something that has lasted so long and has been so successful. But what role does this play in the discussion? What is the balance between our rights and our obligations to one another? And is there a priority system with rights and liberties – are they all equal? I will offer up my thoughts on these issues using examples.

This one book cannot be a panacea to such a profound bundle of complex issues. But it can perhaps convey the story behind the statistics and help dispel some of the myths and biases which impede our discussion. Hopefully, the framework for any discussion on violence in America will focus on our humanity and the stories behind the decisions we make. We are at our best when we care for the least among us. Two groups especially, people at-risk of suicide and young adults, represent the most vulnerable members of our society. We have to make a safe place for them. Our future depends on it.

New York City, March 14, 2013

Section One: Defining the problem; an overview of homicide and suicide in America

As timely and important as this topic seems to us today, it certainly is not new. Statistics vary, but according to the National Center for Injury Prevention and Control, between 2001 and 2010, a total of 306,946 people died of gunshot injuries in the United States. That number includes both homicide and suicide. It means we average over 30,000 gun deaths per year, a number shocking by comparison to any other developed country. In roughly the same period, only about 3 percent of that number of Americans has died in the War on Terror. Yet consider the enormous difference in time, energy and money we spent on both problems.

In 2010 alone, according to the Centers for Disease Control (CDC), there were 19,392 firearm-related suicide deaths and 11,078 firearm-related homicide deaths in America. Plus another seventy five thousand or so shootings that did not result in death, which is a compliment not to our culture but to the emergency medical community.

With numbers of this magnitude, we have some important questions to ask and big decisions to make. As a country, we should be very clear whether we want to continue down this path. It speaks to how we wish to live together as a people. This is our choice as a society, and we need the clearest illumination of the problem and some real solutions if we can have any chance of controlling where we are going. Yet just outlining statistics doesn't help us to see the real problem in all its complexity. These numbers don't mean anything if not given context.

This book seeks to humanize the story of people facing violence in America. Too often, when one hears these subjects talked about on TV or in the press, it seems the speakers are always trying to dehumanize the participants. Either they talk around the people factor with a focus on statistics or weapon capacities. Or else they talk about people by using labels. Calling someone hippie, redneck, gang banger, separatist, drug dealer, good guy, bad guy – these are all just ways of dehumanizing someone and boxing them into a category rather than viewing them as a person. It increases the "otherness" of someone we perhaps don't want to understand. It doesn't help us get to the human dimension of our problems. Easy to dismiss a dead black kid on the streets of Philadelphia as just one less gang banger. But one man's gang banger is really just someone else's kid, a teenager who maybe could have used a little more adult supervision. And the person another might call a redneck is really someone's dad, a guy with a perspective and a story that needs hearing too. Each of the parties to this debate on violence in America has a story to tell. Each is a real human being. Where we go wrong from the very start is to frame this discussion in terms of pejoratives – boxing each other in with labels, or by reducing human lives to statistics and thereby missing the point entirely. Statistics and gun capacities have their place, but first and foremost come human beings.

1.

Guns in the wrong hands

I started this book as a personal journey of inquiry which led me to certain conclusions, and one of them is that guns are getting in the wrong hands. But did the data confirm or deny those conclusions? Like any person, I have come to my own personal set of opinions through a lot of living (57 years now, and counting). My experiences and the experiences of those around me have shaped my thinking. But since one man's opinion can be skewed, I have tried to test my opinions against the greater body of research to see if my conclusions bear up under scrutiny, or need to be revisited. To augment my work, I have also included other people's stories as anecdotes to illustrate and personalize the stories we too often hear as a statistic.

Jury Experience

First, let's start with my story. In New York City, where I live, we do a lot of jury duty. It's due to the presence of so many layers of courts – local, county, state and federal – all on one island. We have appellate courts, supreme courts and courts of international trade. There are family courts, civil courts, criminal courts, juvenile courts, immigration courts. It's almost an industry unto itself. And most of them need jurors who can commute easily. Perhaps someone who lives in the Adirondacks at the other end of the state probably doesn't have to serve much. When I lived in Upstate New York for more than a decade, I only got called once – in Madison County. But here in Manhattan, it is a regular biannual affair.

During my many jury experiences therefore, I have gained an insight into felony crime and the role of guns on our streets. It's not my only source of personal experience, as you'll see later from the personal stories and anecdotes in the following chapters, but it's a good place to start.

As any trial unfolds and evidence is presented, one gets to know the players a little and the thinking going on as they edged toward trouble. Bad moments in human lives, much like plane accidents, usually have an enormous number of antecedents. Rarely does one factor cause the downfall of any complex system, aircraft or human being. And it would be an injustice to oversimplify. But there are some commonalities.

First and foremost, one cannot help but be appalled at the number of youth brought before us. Coming before juries during felony trials, one doesn't seem to see old assailants. Physical violence seems to be the domain of young adults. And because other implements of violence do not cause as much permanent injury or loss of life, firearms are the main instrument of violence which lead these young people to their sad condition in court. The statistics confirm this observation;

> 1.   CNN reports that every single day in the United States, 13 young people below the ages of 24 are the victims of homicide, according to federal data. More than 80 percent are killed with a firearm.
> 2.   In Philadelphia, the majority of homicide victims are African-Americans between the ages of 15 and 24. "Every time there is a loss of life, we have to remind ourselves that these are often children. And we have to ask ourselves where have we failed to protect this child?" said John Rich, director of the Center for Nonviolence and Social Justice at Drexel University.
> 3.   The CDC reports "In 2001, homicide was the second leading cause of death and suicide the third for persons 15–24 years of age. Approximately 60

percent of all homicides and suicides in the United States are committed with a firearm".

The second commonality is that these young adults will permanently pay for this split second decision simply because a gun was involved. At the worst moment in their lives, when their decision making was at its most faulty, the presence and lethality of guns made their momentary mistakes permanent.

And lastly, nothing adequate was being done by society for these young people prior to their crime when they were still out on the streets. But as soon as something went wrong, an overwhelming force was brought against them by a society determined to prosecute and incarcerate them. What a misapplied set of resources. Here is one example.

Anecdote 1: teenagers and guns in the inner city (told by Chris Johnson)

In the fall of 2011, I served on a Grand Jury as Foreman. Under New York State law, unless the defendant consents, all felony cases must be presented to a Grand Jury. Not yet a trial, a Grand Jury is a group of 23 citizens who sit and hear evidence in a multitude of cases and then vote whether to indict or not (majority rules). In our month long service, we heard more than two dozen different felony cases. All but two included firearms as a part of or central to the crime. All included broken lives, violent deaths, pain and suffering for those involved, and ever so many bad choices. At times it became overwhelming to hear. Normally, the evidence was presented by witnesses, or by taped phone calls or video evidence. Occasionally, we heard directly from a participant in the crime.

In most circumstances, like at an office or a school, one would expect a group of people who spend a month together to begin developing bonds. You'd imagine they would start to lunch together or meet for coffee beforehand. You might expect lively conversation at quitting time, as they moved toward the elevator banks, discussing their different evening or weekend plans. Sadly, we didn't do that. So sobering were the cases, that we often spent our time in silence. Two dozen people, standing in mute contemplation, waiting for the elevator. When we disbanded at month's end, there were no long goodbyes or a post rendezvous in a neighborhood bar for a quick drink. We all just left. I was the last in the building, completing paperwork on a particularly egregious home invasion case. Children having been awakened with a gun in their face, then chained to a radiator. So stressed by the experience, the mother's boyfriend later left her for good, unable to sleep in the same apartment. Ripples of pain and suffering spreading out from one event.

Among the many cases, some stand out more than others. I can still remember one witness I swore in as foreman. We sat in an amphitheater like space, with the witness at the bottom, and rings of jurors rising above them leading up to a high table with myself at the center, flanked by the clerk and assistant foreman. Because of the sloping room, I must have sat a good eight feet above the witness table. To the witness, it must have felt like looking up at the high court of heaven sitting in judgment. "Do you solemnly swear . . . " I'd begin while looking into their eyes. Seasoned detectives, who did this for a living, were on autopilot. No discernible response to my words. But to most witnesses, like this one, it was clearly intimidating – a space they weren't prepared for. It was so deeply human to see them at their most vulnerable, and at times difficult to maintain eye contact.

This young man was testifying as part of his own plea deal. He had been part of a small gang whose older members were involved in a shooting. His evidence was intended to catch bigger fish – part of a conspiracy trial we were working on. He was just 17. The Assistant District Attorney (ADA) put questions to him, and his answers were meekly spoken but clear. No embellishment. He kept to the facts. He talked about the presence of guns in his group, how they often kept them under the jackets of the girls that hung out with them in case the police stopped and frisked the gang members. Other guns, usually the larger ones, they kept at somebody's grandmother's apartment. She didn't know, he thought. When asked why his group got the guns, he said that they had heard the gang 15 blocks up the street had purchased some guns and rumor was they'd used one. So, he said, their group had a meeting and decided they should get guns too. A decision clearly based on perceived need for safety and a belief that guns provided that safety. Yet instead of achieving those aims, it led to an arms race, neighborhood style.

The group made the decision that Virginia was the place to buy guns. And as makes sense to teenagers, they stole a car to get there, then went to a gun show and successfully obtained what they wanted. We heard further details from the Virginia detective flown up to NY to testify. When he saw two teenage kids driving a $132,000 Mercedes up I-95 at 100 miles per hour, he knew his arrest record would be good that month. After pulling them over for speeding, he determined the car was reported stolen and arrested them. When they were being booked and their possessions inventoried for storage, they found the guns. Two young lives now toast. Young lives, abandoned to the streets with no help from the system while they were free, but now having been caught, the entire weight of society gets thrown against them. Surely an imbalance of applied resources one could ever imagine.

And yet back in New York, nothing had changed. The perceived threat to the gang was still present. Yet another group meeting was held, and the elders (20 and 22) decided another trip out of state was too dangerous. Therefore they decided to buy through the black market here in the city. Through this, they were able to obtain several hand guns, a semi-automatic hand gun and one assault rifle. They had no clue what they needed, but the guy who sold them said this was the required mix. Like getting pharmacological advice from your meth dealer.

Determining if a gun is operational and loaded is one critical step toward applying New York's various gun laws. A functioning and loaded weapon raises the threat level and consequently the crime that can be charged. So the last bit of questioning of our 17-year-old witness involved ascertaining the conditions of the guns as bought on the black market locally. So as not to be visible from the street, he told us, they had taken them up to the roof of a five story walk up and were showing them around the group. Teen age boys showing off new toys. Might as well be a new X-box. The ADA asked about the assault rifle – was it operational? Yes, he replied. How do you know?, asked the ADA. Tommy fired off a few rounds, he replied. It was a quiet moment of contemplation for all of us. In the middle of the most densely populated area of our country, with the added elevation of a roof top, someone thought it appropriate to fire off a few rounds into the night. That some little girl doing her homework 7 blocks away wasn't turned into jelly was just luck. Young men, acting out, trying to be cool, exercising little or no judgment, blind to consequences, only empowered by their new toys. Teenage angst, assuaged by a false sense of power. Fear turning into a path of evil. The curse of the Ring of Sauron. To touch it is to be seduced by it. A shot like that could travel erratically up to a mile into the night. I went home that evening and did a Google Map search on the site of the test firing. I live just 0.9 miles away.

2.

Gangs, guns and violence

Gangs and their prevalence among America's youth play a principal role in crime in the United States. While violent crime and property crime rates have declined by about 20 percent across the country over the past decade (FBI, 2011; Truman, 2011), gang violence remains high or in some cases is increasing. Estimates vary, but studies have shown that while only a tiny fraction of male youths are members of gangs, they represent the majority of all violent and drug related crimes (FBI). The National Gang Intelligence Center calculates that gangs are responsible for an average of 48 percent of violent crime in most jurisdictions and up to 90 percent in several others. Clearly we must do something about this. As with all other topics in this book, we need to approach it by trying to understand the humanity of the problem.

Who, in fact, is a gang member? Predominantly made up of young people at the high risk age group of 15-24, gang members have an average age of slightly less than 18. The median age for joining gangs has been shown in several studies to be about 14. Gang members are much more likely than non-gang members to possess semi automatic weapons. As one study from the Justice Department shows, "gang members are far more likely to commit certain crimes, such as auto theft; theft; assaulting rivals; carrying concealed weapons in school; using, selling and stealing drugs; intimidating or assaulting victims and witnesses; and participating in drive-by shootings and homicides than non-gang youths, even though the latter may have grown up under similar circumstances."

So it isn't necessarily the person, but the gang environment that causes much of the problem. Therefore, without understanding gangs and why people join them, we will never be able to contain violent crime. Once again, it's the humanity of the situation, not just the guns.

According to research, the most common age that young people start associating or 'hanging out' with gangs is around 13. It's the time they are first lured into that lifestyle and it is their most at-risk moment. If a young person is to be kept out of a gang, 13 is the key age to intervene. Unfortunately, the second and most frequent opportunity for intervention, from the state's perspective, is usually with the first arrest, often in the first 2 years of gang involvement. This is often the first moment the state "meets" the gang member. Typically, these first arrests involve gateway crimes (like property crimes), not yet involving violence, and give the state, if it avails itself, an opportunity to "divert young offenders from the gang subculture before they further endanger their own lives and victimize other citizens." (DOJ).

So why do people join gangs? The reasons are many. "Safety" is a big one. "Feeling unsafe at school may predict gang involvement, as students who feel vulnerable at school may seek protection in gangs" (Gang Problems and Gang Programs in a National Sample of Schools, Gottfredson Associates, 2011). Another study from Pierce College supports this, "Many of these young people feel they need to join a gang to be protected from another gang who controls the area where they live." There also appears to be a high correlation to whether someone witnessed gun violence or not. A study done by the Center for Court Innovation showed that "56 percent of respondents who reported prior exposure to gun violence agreed with the statement, 'In this neighborhood, it is sometimes necessary to carry a gun to protect yourself or your family,' compared with only 33 percent of those not exposed to gun violence.

Respondents exposed to gun violence were also more likely to support the legitimacy of gang membership (31 percent vs. 23 percent). While these results may at first seem counter-intuitive, previous research suggests that fear, which may be triggered by exposure to violence, is associated with support for gun ownership and use among minority youth (Cook et al., 2000)." It is ironic, then, that both the gang member and the legal gun owner, as we will later see, make their decisions predominantly for the same reason – safety. And yet, their actions put both of them at more risk rather than less. Is there an educational opportunity here? Certainly, the availability of guns is like pouring gasoline on an already burning fire.

Finding a place to "belong" is another reason people join gangs. The aforementioned paper from Pierce College suggests, "With many low-income households, there lacks some closeness that individuals need to feel loved. So because gangs offer a sense of closeness, many of these boys decide to join because they are welcomed and are shown love." Many young people who join gangs have a destructive home life either without adequate supervision or an abusive parent. The gang becomes a surrogate family. In many cases, depression or failure at school can also cause a sense of helplessness or disenfranchisement from the possibilities offered by their education system or society in general. A young person might imagine the American dream is not available to them because of their circumstances. This can be a failure to understand their options. They might seek human needs (economic, social and safety) elsewhere through the only avenues they perceive to be open to them. An educational opportunity exists therefore to promote alternatives to gang membership.

Resistance to joining a gang, one might think, would be a difficult challenge for any young person. However, the statistics show something quite different. In the same at-risk environment, youths who choose not to join a gang do not necessarily suffer any adverse consequences, and in fact, in the long run are safer than had they joined. A National

Institute of Justice report concurs, stating that "reality differs dramatically from the intuitive beliefs held by many young people. Clearly, the cost-benefit ratio favors gang resistance, especially if one resists politely, without 'disrespecting' the gang or its members. In instances in which youths resisted gang overtures and suffered physical reprisals, their injuries were seldom serious. Media accounts of gang killings and serious assaults on youths who refuse to join the gang paint an exaggerated picture. The reality is quite the opposite."

So what is the solution here? Decades of addressing the problem piece meal have produced mixed results. But a broad comprehensive approach seems to work best.

The *NY Times* reports that New York's Police Department has a Juvenile Robbery Intervention Program which actively tries to track young teens in an effort to keep them from ever getting into trouble. By tracing Facebook and Twitter accounts, learning their street names and hang outs, the police are ever-present in these young people's lives making it hard for them to become part of a gang.

The Times defines this as "a novel approach to deter juvenile robbers, essentially staging interventions and force-feeding outreach in an effort to stem a tide of robberies by dissuading those most likely to commit them. Officers not only make repeated drop-ins at homes and schools, but they also drive up to the teenagers in the streets, shouting out friendly hellos, in front of their friends. The force's Intelligence Division also deciphers each teenager's street name and gang affiliation. Detectives compile a binder on each teenager that includes photos from Facebook and arrest photos of the teenager's associates, not unlike the flow charts generated by law enforcement officials to track organized crime. The idea, in part, is to isolate these teenagers from the peers with whom they commit crimes — to make them radioactive. "

This program is novel in US law enforcement and deserves support and replication. Not only does it deter gang membership but the data learned will help us discern youthful motivations across the board. Adolescents are the least likely to make good judgments, especially when it comes to powerful firearms, and the more we can understand these young people and find ways to keep these weapons out of their hands, the better. But there are other issues at work here, like disenfranchisement, the need for belonging and surrogate family issues. As these are more complex, first hand data about people's real lives can certainly help us to craft programs which will help "break the trajectory of those born into poverty and neglect, and winding up behind bars before their 18th birthday" (Lieutenant Glassberg, NYPD).

Certainly, for inner city youth in Latino and black populations, one contributing factor to gang involvement is the apparent barriers to entry to the American dream. While 2012 jobless rates for all teenagers is about 23 percent, according to the Department of Labor, 31 percent of teenage Latinos were unemployed and for Blacks of the same age, unemployment was over 40 percent. Certainly, rather than the American dream, it becomes the American nightmare. It has to become a priority to show these young people that an education and staying out of gangs are pathways to a bright future. Yet, all too often they don't see it. People become disenfranchised from the system and drop out. "Ninety-four percent of murder victims under the age of 25 are dropouts", according to San Francisco District Attorney Kamala Harris. And dropouts, if they get to grow up, are more likely to be unemployed, homeless, on welfare or in jail. The cost to society is staggering. Rather than throwing away these young people, we should try to intervene when it matters, on or before the age of 13.

Back in 1997, the Department of Justice produced something called the National Juvenile Justice Action Plan. The Action Plan supports a broad array of proposals including "strong measures to prevent juveniles from using guns illegally and to remove guns from schools through youth-focused community oriented policing, reducing the availability of firearms to youth, strengthening anti-drug and anti-gang measures, and building healthy communities through expanded youth opportunities." Noble goals we have yet to achieve. Overall, dropout rates and violence across America have fallen. But teenage dropout rates remain high and gangs are still prevalent.

Yet people *are* trying. One NYC program that has received some notoriety is SNUG ("Guns" spelled backwards), administered by the New York City Mission Society. From their web site, "What if gun and gang violence really were an epidemic—and spread like one? And what if its spread could be prevented? That is the premise of Operation SNUG, a replication of the highly effective CeaseFire Chicago model. Employing street-credible 'violence interrupters', the program seeks to prevent the spread of violence in Central Harlem by persuading those who are most likely to engage in it to find peaceful solutions to conflict. The program has won the support of, and collaborates with, the Central Harlem community, including religious leaders, the police and the public. Since its inception, the program has mediated more than 50 conflicts that could have resulted in gun violence."

This success is supported by The Department of Justice in the Comprehensive Gang Prevention, Intervention and Suppression Model. "Recent evaluations of the Comprehensive Gang Prevention, Intervention and Suppression Model have shown substantial positive outcomes. Although results are mixed, when the necessary assessment and planning steps were followed in three sites, the Model effectively guided these communities in developing services and strategies that contributed to reductions in both gang violence in all three of the sites and drug-related offenses in two of them."

It seems a comprehensive approach of job opportunity, non violence coaching, educational encouragement, intervention to prevent or suppress gang activity, and concerted efforts to keep firearms out of the hands of our youth, work best only when part of a total big picture approach. Collaboration with community leaders, educators, police and district attorneys and religious leaders is key as part of a total concept involving changing community norms and perceptions of other options to violence.

The most famous example of this strategy, continually sited and replicated, is Cure Violence (formerly CeaseFire) which is a anti-violence program based on the idea that violence is a public health issue which can be prevented by changing behavioral norms. The Department of Justice commissioned an evaluation of this group in 2008 and concluded "There were significant shifts in gang homicide patterns in most of these areas due to the program, including declines in gang involvement in homicide and retaliatory killings."

Another group which replicates Chicago Ceasefire, called Save our Streets (SOS), uses "violence interrupters" (often former gang members themselves) in the New York City neighborhood of Crown Heights.   Marlon Peterson is a coordinator for the group, who says they use personal intervention with high risk people to try to prevent conflicts that could escalate into gun violence. They have had some success, confirmed in the report, "*Testing a Public Health Approach to Gun Violence*," conducted by the Center for Court Innovation, which shows that comparison neighborhoods had 20 percent higher rates of gun violence than the SOS neighborhood did.

Peterson underscored how much poverty contributes to crime. "It's the situation, the environment that's really fueling the problem," Peterson said. "When you have people who don't have access to, you know, first-class education, you have high unemployment. People have been poor for generations. Then you add access to a lot of negative things like guns and you have a lot of people that resort to violence unnecessarily", he says. Peterson feels there are too many guns around. He puts it this way, "If the conversation in DC revolves around the Second Amendment, I would say that Red Coats aren't coming any more so we don't need to hold all these guns".

While not without its detractors – partly because their employees include ex-felons – these kinds of programs do have their supporters including Manhattan Borough President Scott M. Stringer who, in September 2011, called for pilot versions of Operation Ceasefire in all of New York's five boroughs. Newark Police Director Garry McCarthy calls Ceasefire "the next step in the evolution of policing because it's proactive instead of reactive and involves the entire community. The program," he said, "could improve the department's strained relationship with residents by reducing stop and frisk tactics that sometimes make residents feel like the police are an 'occupation force.'"

We don't have to be ex-felons to have conversations with our youth. Parents and teachers play an enormously profound role in setting the tone for civil behavior. In my next anecdote, I address an old but tested teaching vehicle – Shakespeare. In 2009, Jacqui O'Hanlon, Director of Education for the Royal Shakespeare Company wrote "we know (because teachers and students tell us and evaluators document it) that when students engage actively with (Shakespeare's) plays, when they are up on their feet saying the words and making choices about character motivation and setting, they are also exploring living dilemmas about democracy, leadership, family loyalty, love and power. They increase their confidence, self-esteem and communication skills in the process." Wouldn't it be far better if their confidence and self-esteem came from lessons learned from within rather than externalities like weapons? Here are some key themes from one of the bard's best.

Anecdote 2: The lessons of Romeo & Juliet

Most of us first met Shakespeare when we were 14. That's about the time they teach us "Romeo & Juliet" in school. Some would say it's because of the romance of two teenage lovers that is sure to catch the appeal of young people. Doesn't sex always help sell anything – from toothpaste to great literature? But one of its critical advantages is the opportunity to discuss with young people the affects of violence in society and also of gangs. In fact, in "West Side Story", Leonard Bernstein's version, he portrayed the two families as gangs – the Sharks and the Jets. Both works contain themes of pride and 'group think' which distort decision making and produce fatal consequences. And the expanded ripples of impact from each choice spread the affects to so many others in terrible ways.

Let's recap, for those of you who may have forgotten your high school Shakespeare. From the very first scenes we see that the historic city of Verona was rife with violence. Two key local families are locked in a long standing feud. "From ancient grudge break to new mutiny, Where civil blood makes civil hands unclean" (Prologue. 3-4)." It is summer and Verona's streets are filled with fighting ("For now, these hot days, is the mad blood stirring." ACT III SCENE I). The play shows the influence this has on everyone by examining the lives of two particular young people – Romeo and Juliet. It is almost the model for the personal narratives in this book.

As each act of violence and death takes place, it escalates rather than resolves conflict, laying the seeds for the next act of violence. Instead of solving anything, they only perpetuate and further inflame their enmity for one another's families. Pride is often at the root of this interfamily feud. Shakespeare portrays love as the opposing force to pride suggesting the two cannot exist simultaneously in the same person. For example, Romeo will not fight Tybalt in a duel because Tybalt has gone from being his enemy to the relative of his lover. Yet Mercutio gets himself killed, despite his original goal of peace maker, because he cannot sit by while Romeo refuses to fight. His sense of pride and honor are all inflamed by Tybalt's insults and he goes from peace maker to assailant in moments. Rage wins the day. A turning point in the play, it is the first serious and fatal consequence of the central story. Romeo, then inflamed, kills Tybalt and the whole messy die is cast.

We teach these ancient and enduring stories for their cautionary value. They help us to see the human condition in all its brokenness. First appearing as Pyramus and Thisbe in Roman times, Shakespeare's adaptation of Romeo and Juliet is fundamentally a tragedy of human pride, lightly masked as a love story. It is a warning to us across time that love, irrational and compelling in all its manifestations, can distract us from reason. And pride, the cause of Lucifer's fall from Heaven after all (the ultimate cautionary tale), normally to be avoided, can easily distort our judgment and consume us. The pivotal moment where Tybalt's hate meets Romeo's love demonstrates this vividly, and in two parallel universes, it could go either way. It is the fork in the road of time, taken wrongly. The opposing views are met in this one exchange;

TYBALT: Romeo, the hate I bear thee can afford

   No better term than this,--thou art a villain.

ROMEO: Tybalt, the reason that I have to love thee

   Doth much excuse the appertaining rage

   To such a greeting: villain am I none;

   Therefore farewell; I see thou know'st me not.

If only it had ended there. Words are one thing, swords plunged into flesh another. Romeo cannot reconcile these two conditions, love and hate. "O sweet Juliet, Thy beauty hath made me effeminate And in my temper soften'd valour's steel!" Pride rises up to steel his hand, and by killing Tybalt, Romeo gets himself banished from Verona.

It is important to realize that every one of the dead was a teenager or at best 20, even in the earliest Roman era versions. Yet the adults – the heads of the two families – contributed mightily to the violence by setting the stage with their own bad decisions. It takes the final death of Romeo and Juliet ("Poor sacrifices of our enmity!" ACT V SCENE III), for them to realize it. Their complicity in this ignites the passions of youth and lays the foundation for the ultimate tragedy. Where these young people needed the steady hand and wizened guidance of the adults in their midst, they instead received lessons in hostility. "See, what a scourge is laid upon your hate, That heaven finds means to kill your joys with love", says the Prince.

The primary purpose of this first section is to show the vulnerability of youth as they transition to adulthood and the implied obligation of adults to help shepherd them safely through this most fragile period in their lives. As with Lords Montague and Capulet, we must gaze upon the dead youth lying somewhere in America and ask ourselves; what did we do to contribute to this sorry end and what might we have done to prevent it? "All are punish'd" says the Prince of Verona.

3.

Power that seduces and corrupts the heart

Unlike our Shakespearean characters, modern youth – in fact modern humans of all ages – have some remarkable technology at their disposal, especially when it comes to weapons. As a result, the lethality has increased dramatically from the days of the sword. Yet some of the emotions that lay behind our actions have not changed. Like the two families in Verona, feelings of pride, powerlessness and a need to belong can be motivators in our time too. And they are not just restricted to inner city youths who join gangs. Adults are just as vulnerable to these motives.

Cautionary tales serve as a warning to the listener. And they do not only come from ancient wisdom but can be created anew using forms similar to the ancient myths. They can appear to us in the guise of really good fiction. That doesn't make them any less instructive. One renowned example is the *Lord of the Rings* and it is an appropriate setup to my next anecdote.

J.R.R. Tolkien wrote his famous trilogy between the two wars and he had been very much shaped by his prior experiences as a soldier in World War I. He once wrote, "By 1918 all but one of my close friends were dead." He had no romantic view of war or the power of weaponry. Central to his story's plot is the **Ring of Sauron**, imbued with terrible evil power. One of its greatest powers is a corrupting seduction which lulls the wearer into a sense of control and personal power.

At one point in the story, the character Boromir wants to use the Ring himself in the fight against the Dark Lord. Elrond, the elven Lord replies, "Its strength, Boromir, is too great for anyone to wield at will, save only those who have great power of their own. But for them it holds an even deadlier peril. The very desire of it corrupts the heart. Consider Saruman. If any of the Wise should with this Ring overthrow the Lord of Mordor, using his own arts, he would set himself on Sauron's throne, and yet another Dark Lord would appear. And that is another reason why the Ring should be destroyed: as long as it is in the world it will be a danger even to the Wise. For nothing is evil in the beginning. Even Sauron was not so."

Sadly, with the best of intentions, Boromir is eventually seduced by the temptation of power and tries to take the ring for himself to use against evil. Only the humble hobbit, who has no aspirations for power nor desire to use the ring, runs away with it and ultimately saves the day by destroying it. Boromir spends the rest of his life seeking redemption for his act of weakness.

Tolkien once described this human weakness when confronted by "the Ring's power of lust, that anyone who used it became mastered by it; it was beyond the strength of any will to injure it, cast it away, or neglect it." The ring, therefore, becomes the iconic image of something which is unsafe in human hands. One hears an echo in modern times. "From my cold, dead hands!" said Charlton Heston in May 2000.

Anecdote 3: how guns can change a personality (told by Chris Johnson)

I had a grad school colleague – let's call him Tom – who was a great friend. We were young men, starting out in life, and I think we believed we would remain friends forever. At some point in those early years, Tom pursued a career change into law enforcement and went through some rigorous training.

One presumes he also got a rigorous background check. When he returned to us, an ever present gun returned with him. His training had said that the bad guys have guns so the good guys needed to be armed too. Clearly, he was told, he was a good guy. That 'us versus them' vision of the world began to pervade his speech and thought. And the gun itself was like a new character among our little band of friends. Its impact was palpable. Tom even wore it around his apartment and his change in demeanor was as profound as the affect high heels can have on some women – amazing that such small objects can provide so much psychological empowerment to the wearer.

The job also empowered Tom. His stories became filled with examples of dominance; like his ability to walk into a bank president's office without an appointment ("nothing they could do about it", he'd say) or his ability to drive at high speed in unmarked cars. The whole process was one of seduction to a darker side and was particularly disturbing to his friends. Conversations became more difficult over time and his behavior even seemed threatening at times.

Finally, one day while we were having lunch in Midtown, Tom was telling me of a recent search warrant he'd executed in which the home owner was not at home. I don't know if that's even legal, but he was clearly turned on by the subject and spoke in a derisive way that made the home owner seem like some helpless victim. I was appalled at the nature of the conversation and, along with all the previous conversations, I was running out of patience. I asked what he would do if the home owner had come home during the search. Tom immediately said, "I'd shoot him". I'd had enough. I threw some money on the table and walked out. And sadly, we've never seen each other or spoken since.

*   *   *

After that experience, I have wondered about the empowerment people get from guns. I remember one tape we saw on the Grand Jury where an illegal gun sale was being recorded. The seller handed a piece to the buyer –

both were in their late teens – and the buyer began to hold it, altering his grip to get its feel. It was a semi-automatic handgun. "Makes you feel like a man", the seller said. I remember how important that was to me as a teenager, just becoming something but not yet there, so unsure what it was to be a man. I can remember how exhilarating it was with my first car – a ten year old sports car I bought for $600 – when behind the wheel, I too felt like a man. Oh, the externalities it takes to make us feel good.

In February 2013, the Associated Press wrote an article about gun tourism in Guam. They said that many tourists from Japan, a place where guns are not readily available, come to Guam to shoot a gun at the plentiful shooting ranges available on the island. "It was such a feeling of power," observed Keigo Takizawa. "But," he said, "I still don't think anyone should be allowed to have one of their own." Tetsuo Yamamoto, who runs one of the shooting ranges, says that for the Japanese, guns are both exotic and exhilarating. So exhilarating, we are told, that he sometimes asks his guests to stay around for a while to calm down after they've finished shooting.

In a pro-gun article about women learning to use guns in Austin, TX, Ari Sackett, a newcomer to the world of guns observes, "I'm already less afraid because I know how to operate (a gun). Then, rather than the gun having power over you, you have power over the gun." Is that the seduction talking? Who really has power over whom?

The biggest question is, are we as a species ready for that kind of power? With the best of intentions or not the best, from fear or for pleasure, should human beings possess the power to kill so easily? Or, as the title of this book suggests, are guns unsafe in human hands? As Tolkien wrote, nothing is evil in the beginning. But can it become evil? And do these instruments of death have a seductive hold over their owners that non-gun people simply cannot fathom? Why do they sometimes sound so like Gollum who, as he strokes the Ring of Sauron, whispers "My precious"?

4.

Availability of guns - where do they come

from?

It might seem like a funny incongruity to include a story about a terrorist crisis on another continent in a book about guns and violence in America. But like so many stories in this book, Mali represents a cautionary tale. Ironically, the US was also in control of this one, only we let the moment slip through our fingers. We had a chance to keep a bad situation from getting worse, if we only had restricted the availability of weapons.

Anecdote 4: Pouring gasoline on a fire; the case of Mali and Algeria

The rise of Islamists is an old story now, and has caused far more pain and suffering to everyday Muslims overseas than it has to Americans at home. From Central Asia to North Africa, this radical and intolerant variant on Islamic tradition is unwelcome to most. But still it persists. Like a pillow, you push down on it in one place and it pops up in another. And it seems to feed off failed states like Afghanistan and Mali and Somalia, like the flu which can kill the elderly or a lion who takes down the weakest of the herd. So what's different now? Why did all this flair up recently in Mali and Algeria? In short, it is the increased availability of weapons.

We now know the Arab Spring had unintended consequences, especially in Libya. Countries like Egypt and

Tunisia have millennia of national identity giving them a sense of unity. But Libya was a construct of European colonialism and was a new country, created by foreigners, drawing lines on the map. The identity and loyalty of Libyans was to their clan, not their nation. And there were no national institutions to give stability during the collapse of the central government in the way that Egypt's army gave continuity and control. Weapon caches in Egypt never were open to pilfering, since the Army was always in control of them. But in Libya, the armories were maintained by mercenaries and the weapons themselves just disappeared.

Evidence is scant but some of it is clear and disturbing. It turns out that much of what is being used by Islamists in Mali seems to have come from Libya. And even the raid on the oil refinery in Algeria which caused the death of more than 90 people involved former Libyan arms. In January 2013, the UK newspaper The Guardian reports: "In one striking case, Belgian-manufactured landmines originally supplied to Gaddafi's army appear to have been used by the jihadi militants who attacked BP's In Amenas gas facility in Algeria last week."

During the fall of Gaddafi, Britain, France and the US were perhaps overly focused on securing shoulder-launched anti-aircraft missiles. One can perhaps forgive this error since we were supporting the revolution from the air, so anti-aircraft missiles were perceived to be the greatest threat. But there were impassioned pleas from various non-governmental groups in both the security fields and human rights organizations, telling the US to secure all the other types of weapons. Unfortunately these pleas went unheeded. The Guardian quotes Peter Bouckaert, of Human Rights Watch as saying, "The arrival of new weapons changes the game. One day the rebels fight with AK47s and the next day they show up with anti-aircraft guns and other weapons and it's a completely different conflict.

"In a lot of these conflicts the focus is on the most exotic weapons, whether chemical weapons in Syria or Manpads

[anti-aircraft missiles] in Libya, but we have to go back to Iraq in 2003 and look at the carnage caused by much more conventional weapons in the aftermath of the war.

"Two artillery shells can make a car bomb and there are hundreds of thousands of them missing in Libya. For 10 years the US and its allies lost soldiers in Iraq to the weapons that they failed to secure in 2003, and now the same thing has happened on a more massive scale in Libya."

*   *   *

Our own military's increasing use of exotic weapons perhaps distorts our view, making us blind to the threat of conventional weapons. None the less, failure to identify these threats to law and order and failure to diminish their availability had terrible mortal consequences.

This is a cautionary tale for the future, with strategic implications for our society. That humans find reasons to fight one another is omnipresent throughout history. That will no doubt continue. Yet the availability of weapons changes the lethality and the severity of any conflict. Twice now, we've gotten this wrong in the fight against Islamists. And we keep getting it wrong in our own city streets. Hopefully, it's the last time for both.

Availability of guns in our own country

There is a temptation to think that guns used in crimes come only from illegal sources. That simply isn't true. In fact, 75 percent of all mass shootings in this country involve legally obtained firearms (calculated by *Mother Jones*, February 2013). Yet, with over 300 million guns in this country, availability isn't the problem. Getting good data is.

The Tiahrt Amendments, passed by Congress in 2004, restrict crime gun-trace data (that is, data which shows the origin of guns used in crimes). Tiahrt does this by prohibiting use of data in firearm dealer license revocations and civil law suits. In addition, the law prohibits the Bureau of Alcohol, Tobacco, Firearms and Explosives (ATF) from requiring gun dealers to do a physical inventory of their firearms for compliance inspections and requires the FBI to destroy data from background checks of gun purchasers within 24 hours (John Hopkins School Public Health). Despite a broad push to repeal Tiahrt, it amazingly still exists and yet without the trace data on crimes that were committed, we cannot, as a society, have a rational discussion about gun violence.

The evidence we do have shows just a few disreputable gun dealers are responsible for the majority the illegal guns in this country. Before the Tiahrt Amendment shut down access to trace data, a 1999 United States Senate Report found that one percent of the nation's gun dealers supplied nearly half of the guns traced to crimes in 1998. But there's so much we don't know. Since trace data is now suppressed, and private sales (gun shows, internet, home sales) account for a significant portion of gun transfer of ownership, this enormous gray market, which lies somewhere between the legal and the illegal, is largely unknown. Estimates to its possible size run as high as 40 percent of all sales (U.S. Department of Justice). And this segment – legal but untraced – is growing and yet we don't really have a handle on it.

But what about criminals – where do they get their guns? In a 1997 Survey of State Prison Inmates by the DOJ, they report that among inmates who possessed a gun at the time of their crime, 80 percent came from an informal, untraced and private market (family, friends, a street buy, or another illegal source). Retail stores and pawn shops accounted for only 12 percent. Flea markets and gun shows represented fewer than 2 percent.

Therefore, the unmonitored and uncontrolled private market is the principal source for weapons used in crimes. These markets might include many guns that started their existence in a legal transaction, fully registered with background checks, and used by a law abiding citizen. But they didn't necessarily end there. These unregulated secondary markets make getting a gun easy. And it is that easy availability that puts us most at-risk.

Let us remember that on the same day as the Newtown massacre, there was a similar type incident which took place in a school in China. Twenty-two children were injured there, but none killed, solely because the assailant used a knife and not a gun. Clearly, the difference in weapons used made all the difference. Had guns not been readily available to Adam Lanza, perhaps 27 people would still be alive today.

5.

Legacy Guns

Even if a gun originates with a legal transaction on its very first day, there is a potential that it might later end up in the wrong hands or with the right person at the wrong moment in their lives. This is because guns never die, only people do. Guns become a legacy, passed down from generation to generation. Once a gun is out there, it becomes an eternal threat possibility. Gun control is not gun elimination. A civil war gun can still kill you.

Therefore, the safety of a gun at any moment in time can change, as can its owner. The proposition that a legally purchased firearm belonging to a law abiding gun owner will never become a threat to innocent women and children just isn't true. Forever, as they say, is a very long time. Consider the next two anecdotes.

Anecdote 5: The gun in the closet (told by Chris Johnson)

The fondest memories my brother and I have from our youth were spent in Hillsdale, NY at the country farm house of our great grandfather Theophilus Johnson. He was a school principal in the New York City School System, but he kept a home in Hillsdale as a country getaway and because our family had lived there for generations. In fact, the local rural cemetery has my ancestors buried there from my own father all the way back to William Johnson who was born in 1753. I even have a plot there, just to show you what a role that town plays in our family's hearts.

The old house in Hillsdale was a long and rambling affair, with many changes and additions over the years – the "new part" having been added a hundred years ago. It had lots of little bed rooms, and was the perfect getaway for various members of our extended family. Many aunts, uncles, and cousins used it as well. A cheap holiday for young families. And a healthy escape from city air.

Since my great grandfather had died right before I was born, no one actually lived in the house. It was simply used by the family for holidays. So you never knew who might be there when you arrived. There had been another little house on the property that the family used to rent to Charlie Burch. At some point, the little house was sold to Charlie, but the deal always was, he kept an eye on our house, in case of broken pipes in the winter or some other problem occurred, like a squirrel getting in. He also made sure the driveway was plowed after a storm.

One late night, when I was in high school, my parents and I arrived after a long drive up from Long Island. It was late and we planned to go right to bed. The house was cold as usual and so I elected to sleep in a tiny little room with a single cot sized bed we called "the chimney room", so called because it was nestled behind the main chimney. It was usually the best room to awake in. Come morning, someone other than me, often my brother or my dad who are early risers, would light the first fire of the day and that meant I had the one place you could get up and get dressed in without fear of frostbite.

The "newer part" of the house had thick oak doors, and at some point in my preparations for bed, I noticed what looked to be a bullet hole, right through this massively thick door at waist height. I carefully looked into the hole and saw it went right through the door. Looking around the room, I saw a matching hole in the opposite wall. Had someone been sleeping in the bed, the bullet's trajectory would have crossed inches above their nose. Furthermore, the hole in

*the wall, led into the room my parents were about to sleep in.
I yelled "Dad?!?"*

*After bringing my father up to speed on the mysterious bullet
holes, the two of us tried to trace its path by looking for a
corresponding hole in his room. Just where had this shot
originated, we wondered? However, there was no hole there
and we concluded the bullet had stopped somewhere inside
the intervening wall. So back to the chimney room we went.
In the hope of determining the bullet's origins, logically now
in the other direction, we moved the heavy oak door to look
behind it. And there was another hole proving that the
source must be from the room on the other side – Aunt
Esther's room!*

*A little aside regarding my Great-Aunt Esther. Every family
has its drama and my own has its share. But my Great-
Uncle Murray topped all by divorcing his wife and marrying
his secretary Esther. A scandal worthy of "Mad Men"
maybe, but this happened long before it was fashionably
uncool. On top of it, Murray's first wife was a friend to other
family members and conflict was bound to ensue.*

*For many reasons and a host of incidents that happened
long before my time, eventually a kind of cold war evolved,
and Esther and our family stopped speaking. Murray even
went so far as to build a log cabin a half mile up the hill so
Esther wouldn't have to share the big house with anyone.
We would see Murray from time to time – my brother and I
adored him – but Esther was a stranger to me. I cannot
even conjure up an image of her in my head. Other than at
Murray's funeral, the only time I remember seeing her was
an unexpected moment when they passed us on the
driveway, and she pulled a newspaper over her head so she
didn't have to acknowledge us.*

*And yet, there was a bedroom in the main house still
reserved for her that was off limits and locked. As kids, it
had developed a kind of lore, like Mrs. Havisham's room of
literary fame. One could only imagine what was in there.
But to imagine bullets emerging from a locked room,*

reserved for a strange woman who never stayed there, added greatly to the mystery. My father and I looked at one another and our eyes went wide.

We spent the next hour trying to find a skeleton key that fit her door. The old part of the house where her room was worked on a key system older than Ben Franklin and there were jars of extras laying around. It was always a fun game to play on a rainy weekend – which key went where? But we'd never tried to enter Esther's room. Finally we were successful and with trepidation, we opened the door. There, in fact, was the original bullet hole. But no gun. There was a dusty old bed, covered in some Victorian lace covering, with perhaps 30 old shoes laid out in rows on top. These were shoes of a kind one doesn't see any more – late 19th Century stuff with lace up grommets and buttons. It was a bazaar tableau. One bare and ancient bulb in the ceiling provided the anemic light. We looked around a little, assured ourselves that the threat was over, even if the mystery was not, and relocked the door.

The next day, after breakfast, Charlie Burch came over to say hello. He'd seen us arrive the night before but felt it too late to bother us. My dad started to tell Charlie about the mystery and you could see Charlie's face begin to sag. It took a bit of time, but finally Charlie owned up to the story. He said he was checking the house as was his charge, and he got motivated to look into Esther's room. Apparently he had never been their either. After snooping around, he found a rifle standing upright in the corner of the closet. That guns exist in the country was certainly no surprise to any of us and Murray had always been a hunter and woodsman. But this was unexpected. To get a better look, Charlie took the gun over to the window for more light and for some reason, tested it. To his utter shock and horror, it went off. Damn near scared him to death, he said. Like a startled rabbit, he threw the gun under the bed, locked the door, and high tailed it back to his own house. He didn't even tell his wife. Poor Charlie was owing up to this like a Sunday confession. He seemed surprised when my father and I thought it funny. One part of the mystery solved.

But then the questions began. What to do about the gun now? And what kind of crazy lady would leave a loaded gun in a house famous for its large population of children? No doubt the gun was originally Murray's and purchased legally and properly back in the day. And had Murray known, I'm sure it would have been properly stored too. But Esther was a loose cannon – literally it turns out. And perhaps, at the peak of one of her fights with my family, she sat fuming in her room feeling surrounded by enemies and sought comfort in the ready access of a firearm. Of course, once it was there, she probably didn't know what to do with it. And she hadn't slept in the room in decades. So the problem simply went unresolved. And yet, each of the past three generations of my family had been at-risk, unknowingly. For years, my brother and I and my cousins had played in that house, and gotten into everything we weren't supposed to, like kids do. God knows how we avoided a tragedy.

At that point, Murray was quite elderly and not well. He died shortly thereafter. So my father and Charlie agreed to dispose of the gun without mentioning it. Charlie said he knew a gun dealer and he'd take care of it. And that was that. The gun in the closet, bought legally I'm sure, got caught up in the tensions of family disharmony, which was only one more bad decision away from killing someone in my family. And we never knew it was there.

*   *   *

Anecdote 6: The guns of a dead man; the case of Freddie Fudge (as told by Edwin Garcia, Veteran and NYC resident).

I met Freddie Fudge in 1981. We were both stationed in Fort Bliss in El Paso, Texas. Freddie was in one battery and I was in another, but we still got to know one another. My specialty made it easy to meet people. I worked in personal records, maintaining and reviewing soldiers' records for eligibility for promotion. As a result, I had to interview practically everyone.

Freddie liked excitement and was a fun guy to be with. He loved motorcycles and the whole image that went with them, including the black leather jackets, which he always wore when not in uniform. Freddie also had achieved enough rank and service time whereby he earned the privilege to live off base. That made visiting him even more popular for those of us who lived on base. It was our getaway. His place was our hang out and there was always a group of off duty soldiers there enjoying a few beers.

Living off base allowed Freddie to enjoy his other passion – guns. It seemed like they were under every pillow. Freddie had about 15 including a couple shotguns, a .22, and a 44 magnum that he really liked because of its tremendous kick.

To a guy like me from New York City, this was a new experience. Guns, to my way of thinking, were dangerous and used in crime. At least, that's how I saw it at first. I was so surprised how easy it was in Texas to get a gun and I kept asking him questions. Freddie told me you only needed to be 18 in Texas to own and possess a firearm and you had to have a valid state ID. I turned 18 just before arriving at Fort Bliss, and got my first drivers license and first car in Texas. But I never bought a gun.

I always had respect for weapons. To me, being from New York City, guns were something dangerous to have around. The only people who were supposed to have guns were the police. That's how I was brought up. Of course, as a soldier, I was trained to bear arms, which gave me even more respect. In truth, I was scared what they could do.

At some point, Freddie mentioned going out into the desert and hunting jack rabbits. He described the whole thing enthusiastically, adding that he used a shotgun because "if you hit a jack rabbit with a rifle, you were just lucky". He encouraged me to come along and I did a few times. We'd *drive out East on route 62 and less than an hour from base you quickly came into high desert. We'd park the van and walk in as far as we could. Sometimes there wouldn't be any jack rabbits and we'd just shoot at beer cans. Jack rabbits can be jittery. When you get there, they might show up to investigate something new, but they're easily startled and it didn't take much to send them running.*

One day, Freddie received orders to transfer for a tour in Alaska. That's life in the Army. Later, I'd be transferred to Germany, although I didn't know it yet. When the Army moves you, they handle everything. But they wouldn't move his guns, which created an obvious problem. We talked about it – what to do with them? "Now I gotta get rid of the guns before I leave", he said.

I'm not sure how he did dispose of them, or even if he got around to it. Shortly after our discussion, Freddie had decided to take one more ride with a motorcycle buddy before the Army shipped his bike to Alaska. They were going through an intersection when a drunk driver, going the other way, ran the light. The friend was seriously injured, but Freddie was killed instantly.

I keep thinking about those guns and where they went afterwards – after the original owner is gone? Who knows how his house and his affects were disposed of? The Army would have taken some personal affects and shipped them to his parents, but as to the rest, it's anybody's guess.

*   *   *

The point of both these anecdotes is that guns outlive their owners and all the control at point of purchase and all the banning of new guns will never make the old ones go away. How many guns have gone into dubious hands long after a law abiding owner lost control of them through age, illness or death? The very existence of these legacy weapons can represent a permanent threat to future generations, not necessary because of the original purchaser, but because of a distraught family member or less than law abiding heir.

The numbers of guns we're talking about is enormous. According to ATF reports, in 2010 there were 5,459,240 new firearms manufactured in the United States, 95 percent of which are for the U.S. market. An additional 3,252,404 firearms were imported into the U.S at the same time. That's over 8 million new firearms on the street in just one year.

Yet, if we stopped manufacturing and never made another gun again, the country would still be awash in weapons. The Congressional Research Service estimates that the number of firearms in the U.S. amounts to 310 million units, including 114 million handguns, 110 million rifles, and 86 million shotguns. With an average owner's age in the mid 40's, we can expect within 30 years or less to see the largest transfer of firearms in human history – all through unregulated means via a gray private market. No background checks. No assessment of appropriateness of the buyer. No registration or tracing of any kind. As people age and become less likely to use the weapon for hunting or sport, and have decreased capacity due to health issues, those guns will find a new home – with or without forethought. And those guns don't die of old age, only we do. So what is our plan? Are we thinking about this?

The odds are no one is planning this issue any better than my Great-Uncle Murray or Freddie Fudge. The day we buy a car, we don't think about its disposal either, but unlike guns, cars don't last forever. Cars have a way of taking themselves out of commission. A hundred year old car can't get you to work. But a hundred year old gun can kill you. So the next time you speak with someone who considers themselves a law abiding gun owner, ask them about their legacy plan for these weapons. Like land mines left over from some long forgotten war, old guns can become a profound threat when unleashed upon some unknown future. All this talk of gun control won't make these guns go away. They'll be here for generations. This could be yet another can we kick down the road for our grandchildren to deal with. Or not.

Speaking about weapons reduction of a different kind, Ronald Reagan once said "I can't believe that this world can go on beyond our generation and on down to succeeding generations with this kind of weapon on both sides poised at each other without someday some fool or some maniac or some accident triggering the kind of war that is the end of the line for all of us. And I just think of what a sigh of relief would go up from everyone on this earth if someday–and this is what I have–my hope, way in the back of my head–is that if we start down the road to reduction, maybe one day in doing that, somebody will say, 'Why not all the way? Let's get rid of all these things'."

So, how do we do this? How can we reduce the threat of legacy guns on future generations?

The NRA could provide an enormous service in educating the legal gun owning public to the importance of legacy planning for guns after their lifetimes. After all, we do it for musical instruments, works of art, family bibles and anything else deemed of special value to a family. My own mother and I have had discussions regarding her Steinway grand piano. And everyone should have a will and a living will so that future decisions are made in accordance with your wishes. (Note to reader, if you don't have either a will or living will, put down this book and call an estate attorney right now.)

Perhaps a buyback program could be implemented on a national scale. One that would allow any gun owner, who didn't have someone to leave their guns to (or anyone they wanted to leave them to), the option to leave them in their will to a national buyback program. This would serve two functions; preserving value to their estate and at the same time removing the legacy weapons from possible unintended consequences to future generations. The program might even work as a tax deduction for returned weapons. Buyback programs are often discredited because they appeal to the legal gun owner and not the criminal. But as we've just pointed out, a gun in the hands of a law abiding owner today will not necessarily be in those hands tomorrow.

Regardless of the mechanism, future reduction in the mass availability of arms in this country is in the best interest of our grandchildren's public health. We don't need these weapons killing anyone decades after we're gone. The obligation to plan for the distribution of legacy guns is ours to do in our lifetimes.

6.

Global Arms Trade

The United States is the world's number one weapons dealer with 40% market share for conventional weapons. Although this may not seem like a topic directly impacting violence in America, it is morally related. We would be profoundly disingenuous to worry about firearm deaths in our own country without considering the consequences of US made products killing people in other countries.

And those products are numerous. Globally, there are approximately 639 million small arms and light weapons. Access to these weapons in troubled hot spots has allowed devastating human rights violations in places like Sudan, Syria and Congo. And it is estimated, these guns cause the killing of one person every minute.

In March 2013, at the time of this writing, the UN will hold the final and concluding conference on the Arms Trade Treaty. The United Nations points out that its peacekeeping efforts alone costs the world $7 billion per year, and the global annual burden of armed violence stands at $400 billion. The UN points out, "Without adequate regulation of international arms transfers and high common standards to guide national export decisions, the human tolls and financial costs will remain colossal."

The UN goes on to say, "Virtually all international trade in goods is regulated. But no globally agreed standards exist for the international arms trade." The Arms Trade Treaty would establish high common standards for international trade in conventional arms.

The NRA has taken great measures to oppose this treaty as potentially endangering domestic gun sales. So great has been their opposition, that the Obama administration pulled out of talks on this treaty last summer. The December 2012, *the Hill* reported, "The arms-trade treaty stalled in July, with gun-control activists accusing the Obama administration of sandbagging support for the bill to avoid criticism from Republicans and pro-gun-rights Democrats ahead of the election." Whether that reason is true or not, certainly, this treaty cannot move forward without the largest gun supplier being a party to it now.

It is a frequent bias of America, when considering our public policies that we look only to the consequences for our own people and not for others around the world. Consider the recent debate about whether drones are legal when targeting Americans. The moral issue of killing others does not seem to surface.

How, then, can we live up to our ideals as a people, if we are the foremost global marketers of death? Consider the troubled border towns of northern Mexico, where the vast majority of weapons can be traced back to the US. Mexico has long complained that the United States is responsible for arming the drug cartels resulting in the deaths of more than 47,000 people in the last six years (estimates from Mexico's Attorney General). And the lax weapons laws of Texas, New Mexico and Arizona result in 50 to 100 percent more homicides in cities that border those states than ones that border California with its tighter gun laws. It's obvious where the weapons come from, and if they weren't there, it's also obvious that homicide rates would drop.

So we citizens have skin in this game. We are complicit to violence in countries we might never even visit. And it isn't sufficient to only address violence in America since our gun culture is a contagion causing fatalities in other countries. At the very least, we need to vote in favor of the UN's Arms Trade Treaty. And maybe look ourselves in the mirror.

7.

Bad choices made by good people

The decisions we make define us. The choices we all have available to us at any given moment can be many - sometimes more than we know. Yet the ones we select will shape our future and the future of those around us. Our life experiences, our biases and prejudices, our education, our temperament and more, all combine in how we choose. Maybe we simply don't see all the options open to us. We do know that, in the worst moment of our lives, when we face a situation of extreme import, all humans are capable of choosing wrongly. And in such circumstances, we hope for two things; that we can be forgiven and second that our mistakes hold no permanent consequences. Putting something back together again is, in itself, part of the human journey and part of personal healing. We repair relationships and broken lives, and therein restore ourselves. That is, if what we've broken can still be fixed.

In December 2012, *Huffington Post* quoted Dr. Garen Wintemute, of the University of California, Davis, Medical Center. "The U.S. is not a uniquely violent society," said Wintemute, who practices emergency medicine and conducts research on the nature and prevention of gun violence. "Our overall rates of violence are similar to Australia, Canada and Western Europe. Where the U.S. stands out, is in the homicide rate. That's a weapon effect. It's not clear that guns cause violence, but it's absolutely clear that they change the outcome," said Wintemute.

In the following anecdote, you will hear about Churito, a man faced with an abusive circumstance – terrible to be sure, and he had a choice to make. Unfortunately, he made the worst possible one he could make, in large part because he had access to a gun. It is a simple equation. Bad choices plus availability of guns equals permanently unfixable outcomes. The breach that cannot be repaired. The wound that won't heal.

As humans, we know we will always make mistakes. It is in our nature. So we have to plan for that. It's why we have air bags and guard rails and childproof caps and why pills come in different shapes and colors so we don't mistake one for another. Yet, in an environment where we have ready access to push button death, the potential exists for a mistake that can never be fixed. A decision made that can never be reconsidered. A bridge burned. Here is one such example, which took place not 600 feet from my own apartment building.

Anecdote 7: The choices we make; the case of Churito (as told by Edwin Garcia, Veteran and NYC resident)

By all accounts, Jesus Velazquez was having a tough final few years. Diabetes had left him with both legs amputated. Poverty saw him in a single room occupancy hotel (SRO), where I had a contract to provide some maintenance services – that's how I got to know him. Velazquez, who had worked for 30 years in the garment district, had grown increasingly depressed and started drinking heavily in recent years as a result of his diabetes. He had some prosthetics and a walker, but never really left the building. And he had no family. But New York City is not without its resources and the city's social services system is probably second to none. Between social security, subsidies from the city, food stamps, and a host of other programs, Churito as we called him, was just getting by.

Unfortunately, people like that are often victimized and Churito was no exception. He was harassed, tormented and mugged regularly by Mr. Gonzalez, a 300-pound man with an extensive arrest record for drug dealing, burglary, and robbery. Clearly no addition to any community, Marcelo Gonzalez posed a threat to Churito. So one day, after speaking to Gonzalez, Churito went upstairs to his room – not an easy task with artificial legs and a walker - and returned with a loaded .32-caliber semi-automatic pistol. He walked up to Mr. Gonzalez, who was sitting on the front stoop of the building, and shot him four times in the back and head.

Premeditated murder. Lots of time to reconsider. Clearly a response to rage and frustration. "The reason why I shot him was because I'm an old man and he's been picking on me all the time," he told the police when he was arrested. After a trial and a plea deal to reduce the charges in consideration for his health, Churito was sentenced to 5 to 10 years in prison. He later died there.

*   *   *

My friend Edwin makes it clear in our conversations that "Heavy" as Marcelo Gonzalez was known, was a bad egg. Nobody in the neighborhood was going to miss him. He apparently hit up many at-risk persons as a matter of routine. The issue is not whether Gonzalez needed to be stopped, but how. For reasons known only to Churito, he chose not to seek other alternatives.

We can all imagine getting so angry we want to hurt the guy. But is that the choice we would make? Churito could have called the police. He could have spoken to social workers. He could have spoken to city housing authorities. He could have confided in a priest. He could have dialed 911. All of these options, Edwin says, were available to the people in this SRO. Yet Churito chose a gun.

Neither Edwin nor I know where Churito got the gun, but that doesn't really matter. Regardless of whether it was obtained legally or illegally, or even how long he'd had it, the gun's mere availability changed Churito's options. It gave him the one choice that could not be undone. We don't know if he really weighed those options, because depression and anger can cloud judgment. We do know that if the gun hadn't been there, no one would have died. For the cost of a phone call, the problem could have been solved in other ways.

8.

Suicide as a choice

Sadly, killing others isn't the only bad choice available to people. Killing one's self is an even bigger problem in this country. Statistics show that suicide is the most likely cause of death by gun coming before homicides. In fact, firearm suicides are on the rise, accounting for 16,869 deaths back in 2001 growing to 19,766 in 2011 (CDC). Attempted but unsuccessful suicide rates are even higher still. It is estimated that there are as many as 750,000 suicide attempts each year (suicide.org). This indicates a high failure rate, with dozens of people making the attempt for each successful suicide. Women commit three times as many attempted suicides as men, yet men succeed more often because they use guns as their preferred method. The lethality of guns makes men more likely to succeed at suicide whereas women choose less aggressive solutions which are more prone to failure such as poison or pills.

Yet, this important aspect to the gun debate is not heard often enough. In a January 2013 article about Suicide, the Boston Globe noted that "public health researchers around the country are making the argument that the issue of suicide should be a much larger part of the discussion (on guns). To reduce gun deaths as they really happen, they say, will mean not just fighting crime or keeping firearms out of the hands of potential killers, but trying to minimize the number of people who have access to guns during their darkest hours."

As it regards suicide, does the presence of a gun really endanger the occupants of the house? Why would this be?

The primary explanation is that most suicide attempts are made spontaneously (less than an hour between the decision to kill themselves and the actual attempt). Often the crisis event that prompted the attempt was a momentary non-repeating event (loss of job, relationship problem). This is proven by the fact that 90 percent of people who survive a suicide attempt do not go on to die by suicide. That means they didn't try repeatedly. It is the lethality of guns which makes them more effective and increases the success rate over other attempted suicidal means. Hence, in addition to a person's mental state, the availability of a gun increases the chance of a successful suicide.

Yet, it so rarely comes up in the conversation about gun ownership. We continue to hear about the law abiding gun owner, without considering the effects on their family. *The Boston Globe* goes on to cite several sources, saying "'It's remarkable how many people discount suicide, as if there's nothing that can be done about it,' said John Rosenthal, the Boston developer behind the group Stop Handgun Violence, which funds the antigun billboard on the Mass. Pike. He cited one study suggesting that the vast majority of firearm suicides among youth are committed with guns owned by a family member. 'Talk about low-hanging fruit.'

"But for most people, the possibility that someone they love or they themselves will die by suicide feels much more remote, and less urgent, than the risk of getting shot by an armed robber or a mass murderer like Adam Lanza. As Garen Wintemute, a public health researcher specializing in firearm violence at University of California-Davis, said, 'The debate is focused around the threats that people see to themselves, and that only makes sense.'

"Yet it's important not to lose sight of the fact that, even though large-scale atrocities like Newtown are the ones that force us to confront gun violence as a nation, the opportunity to save lives may be greatest in the steady drip of private tragedies that take place every day—one by one, and out of the public eye."

Anecdote 8: The worst moment in a young man's life (compiled from various news sources)

Kameron Reichert was not a kid you would have suspected of anything so dramatic. A normal 17 year old, with a fondness for his first car, a used Grand Prix. He came from a good family, participated in sports and had an easy time making friends. And yet, it came out later that he had told his friends he was thinking of ending his life. Although he didn't show signs of depression, something was present in his inability to cope. No one noticed how serious it had become.

The young man had a small run in with the law (being caught underage with tobacco products in his car), followed by some mild punishment from his parents (revoked cell phone privileges and limited time with friends). Now Kameron's circumstances might seem mild to us adults, but unfortunately he was unable to put them into perspective. One morning, while his parents were at work, and his sister was a school, Kameron shot himself with a .22-caliber pistol that belonged to his mother's grandfather. He was cold by the time his father found him.

Incredibly, after the suicide, friends and neighbors confided that they too had felt moments of depression. They had even held guns in their hand, they said, contemplating pulling the trigger. While suicide is the No. 3 cause of death among American youth, in Kameron's home state of Wyoming, it ranks second. Wyoming, by the way, is the state with the highest prevalence of households reporting the presence of firearms.

Kameron's crisis was most certainly temporary. Yet his absence is permanent. Incredibly, even after losing a son, Kameron's father still cherishes the family gun collection, and strongly opposes talk of gun control in Washington. "I will always believe in guns," he said.

*   *   *

Part of the problem is a failure to identify the likely profile of the suicide victim. "This doesn't happen to families like us," as Kameron's father pointed out in his 911 call, "I always thought it happens to families who have a lot of family problems." *The Boston Globe* continues with, "We picture turf wars between gangs, abusive husbands turning on their wives, armed robbers punishing their victims, mass murderers opening fire on defenseless people. When we talk about how to reduce gun violence in America, what we overwhelmingly think about is preventing murder. But murder is not the kind of gun violence that kills the most Americans."

The profile of the suicide candidate is key to understanding who is at-risk. According to data from the Centers for Disease Control and Prevention (CDC), suicides affect mostly older populations and predominantly are among white persons. In fact, 80 percent of all firearm suicide deaths were by white males (Firearm & Injury Center at Penn). Suicides are most likely to occur in the South. Interestingly, these are coincidentally the same profiles as persons who own a gun and in the same region with the highest rate of gun ownership and gun violence (assault deaths per 100,000 are 67 percent higher in the southern states than in the northeast). While coincidence does not necessarily guarantee causality, a number of sources do indicate that there is a relationship between a state's gun ownership rates and suicide rates. In states with the highest rate of gun ownership, the suicide by firearm rate increases dramatically as compared to states with the lowest gun ownership, whereas the non-firearm suicide rate does not vary at all (CDC).

According to a 2008 report from the *New England Journal of Medicine*, "The empirical evidence linking suicide risk in the United States to the presence of firearms in the home is compelling. There are at least a dozen U.S. case–control studies in the peer-reviewed literature, all of which have found that a gun in the home is associated with an increased risk of suicide. The increase in risk is large, typically 2 to 10 times that in homes without guns, depending on the sample population (e.g., adolescents vs. older adults) and on the way in which the firearms were stored."

In February of 2013, the Psychiatrist Jeffrey Freedman wrote in the *NY Times*, "Since suicidal behavior often has an impulsive component, those who are more determined can be saved if the method is made more difficult. This can be aided by reduced access to guns. "

This is supported further in the simplified summary found on www.suicide.org , "Note that firearms are, by far, the most common method for suicide (55 percent of all suicides are completed with a firearm). Thus it is imperative that a suicidal person not have access to a firearm."

The *New York Times*, in a February 13, 2013 article, seems to think so too. They state, "Most researchers say the weight of evidence from multiple studies is that guns in the home increase the risk of suicide. 'The literature suggests that having a gun in your home to protect your family is like bringing a time bomb into your house,' said Dr. Mark Rosenberg, an epidemiologist who helped establish the C.D.C.'s National Center for Injury Prevention and Control. 'Instead of protecting you, it's more likely to blow up.' "

However, *the Times* also points out that there could be other factors. "Gary Kleck, a professor of criminology at Florida State University in Tallahassee, contends that gun owners may have qualities that make them more susceptible to suicide. They may be more likely to see the world as a hostile place, or to blame themselves when things go wrong, a dark side of self-reliance."

The Times goes on to point out, "Reducing access to lethal means has worked in other countries. An intervention in Israel preventing soldiers from taking their guns home on weekend leave, a time when many soldiers' suicides occurred, helped reduce the suicide rate among them by 40 percent."

The lesson we learn here is; the presence of a gun increases the chance of a lethal outcome – in this case, a successful suicide. Whether we ever get a handle on the causes of suicidal tendencies and the early identification of persons most at-risk, the means by which suicides are accomplished is something we understand completely. And the most effective step we can take to reduce those suicides is to prevent access to a firearm at that moment of crisis.

9.

Social and financial costs

The statistics are bad enough – there are more than 75,000 non-fatal shootings each year in the US. And firearm injuries from these shootings disproportionately affect young people (Firearm & Injury Center at Penn). Among the leading causes of death for those aged 15-24, homicide ranks second and suicide ranks third, with the number of firearm related homicides and suicides outnumbering the next nine leading causes of death combined.

But these violent events themselves are further magnified by the costs to our broader society, both social and monetary. Each violent act results in lives cut short or forever impacted by that violence with ripples spreading outward to an ever larger number of affected individuals. So it's not just someone else's problem. The expanded ripple effect to American society extends this pain and suffering to hundreds of persons impacted by each violent event, which ultimately affects tens of millions of us.

Consider the next story and its impact on a broader community.

Anecdote 9: the things we do when we're young (compiled from various news sources)

Mario, 16, like most young men, likes to play basketball. Orlando's Willie Mays Park, where he goes to play, is in a residential neighborhood and provides the community with green space and a variety of recreational opportunities like basketball. In the afternoons after school, you can find young people enjoying their free time and great Florida weather. As a result, Mario was a daily visitor to the park.

There's another young man who also comes to the park. Only his choices aren't as simple as Mario's who is only looking for a little recreation. To this other young man, who is 17, one day it somehow seems appropriate for him to bring a gun to the park. No indication he wanted to use it. Maybe it made him feel cool? Or empowered? All we know is, his bad choice – unthinkable to the rest of us - is clearly the stuff of youth. An adult would know better. Tucked inside this fellow's waistband are the lethal ingredients of a tragedy.

It's just another Monday afternoon in January – mild in that part of the world - a pleasant evening to play basketball, in the mid 70's with partly cloudy skies. While playing a game (with the gun still in his waistband), he gets jostled and bumped by other players – a normal occurrence for this sport. As a consequence, he chooses to remove the gun to check it and it goes off accidentally. In a crowded park on a crowded court, he was bound to hit someone. That someone was Mario.

Laying on the ground, Mario's brother comforts him as they wait for the ambulance. It's a terrifying moment especially because it was so unexpected. No fight preceded it. No arguments. No warning. The doctors later do what they can, but the bullet is lodged in his spine and Mario is left paralyzed from the waist-down. It may have been an accident, but the 17 year old shooter is charged with carrying a concealed firearm, improper exhibition of a dangerous firearm, discharging firearm in public, possession of a firearm by a minor and culpable negligence causing injury.

*   *   *

I read about these two young men, and I can't help but count the victims. Surely, there is Mario himself, who will now spend a lifetime with disability. There is his mother who was on video struggling with her faith to forgive and praying for a miracle for her son's recovery. He had dreams of entering the military, she said, now dashed unless the paralysis changes. There is his brother who held his hand while they waited for an ambulance and will no doubt have those memories his whole life. Mario's whole extended family, friends and neighbors will suffer from lost youth and lost mobility of this young man.

Then there are the many people who were at the game. It is said there was a crowd. This was their park. Normally, a place of safety for children to be children. Even Mario said later to his brother, he no longer wanted to go back there. A wounded neighborhood. How many people fled the scene, not knowing why bullets were flying? How many others in that neighborhood will change their behavior forever – keep their kids out of the park or take other steps because they are now afraid? Will someone else obtain a firearm? Fear is toxic and contagious and does not dissipate quickly.

Let's not forget the law enforcement officials. Try to imagine if your job meant getting a call that a gun went off in a crowded park and it was you who were supposed to take care of it! Like firemen who run toward a burning building, the police have to run toward the guy with the gun. What stress do they feel? And their families? If you heard that story on the evening news and your daughter was a cop, what then? Pain, spreading out like a tsunami following an earthquake.

Then there is the medical staff. In the case of Mario, how stressful is it to try to remove a bullet embedded near the spine? And then to fail? To then have to go explain to the mother?

And of course, there is the shooter himself. His life is changed forever. A decision to carry a gun, not use it, but just to carry it, will scar him for life. A choice made in youth will cost him for decades. The National Corrections Reporting Program indicates that roughly half of all prison inmates in the US enter the system below the age of 30. But with sentences getting longer (because of mandatory minimum sentences, three strikes laws, and an increase in the number of crimes punished with life and life without parole), the old age of our prison population (persons over 50) has become the fastest growing segment. And for prisoners who were age 51 or older, 40.6 percent were serving sentences of more than 20 years or life sentences. So we have people my age sitting in prison paying for a crime of their youth, long after they pose a threat to society, now at an age in which they would never commit the bad choices they once made. What is the cost of these lost lives? With the world's largest jail and prison population, the US is paying a considerable cost indeed, social and financial.

Then there are the families of these persons. What cost there? How does a crime like this affect younger siblings of the shooter? And the parents? And girlfriends/boyfriends, or perhaps the shooter's own children? Each of these parties suffers from the incident as well, paying emotionally of course and financially if the incarcerated person is a bread winner. And they often pay with time, spent on trials and prison visits.

Ripples upon ripples, spreading ever outward, from this single moment in time. Perhaps as many as a thousand people could be forever altered by this one bullet. What is the cost to society, not only to the lives lost and lives spent idle in jail, but to the countless numbers of people irrevocably affected by the event?

Just as important as the social impact, is the monetary costs to society - victim costs, criminal justice system costs, lost productivity estimates for both the victim and the assailant – which in total can be enormous. In 2007, the National Institute of Health estimated that criminal offenses resulted in approximately $15 billion in economic losses to the victims and $179 billion in direct government expenditures on police protection, judicial and legal activities and incarceration.

Then there are the indirect costs of lost productivity of both the shooter and the victim – in the hundreds of billions. Researchers at Iowa State University, led by sociologist Matt DeLisi, put the direct and indirect costs to society of each murder at $17,252,656. The biggest component is prison costs. According to the Pew Economic Mobility Project, the federal, state and local governments spend more than $50 billion a year on jails and prisons.

Mark Cohen comes up with similar numbers in his 1998 landmark paper "The Monetary Value of Saving a High-Risk Youth" estimating that preventing a young offender from going into a life of crime might save society $1.7 million to $2.3 million—encouraging states and local governments to spend more on prevention programs for violent children and teens.

The Rand Corporation 2011 study "*Save Money Hire Police*" states, "The high cost of crime to society suggests that adding police officers (in particularly understaffed police departments) may give large cities a sizable return on their investments."

The point of each of these studies is that money and time spent up front before the person makes a bad choice are financially so much cheaper than the high costs to society after the fact. In this case, prevention is the cure. And it's cheaper too.

Programs like the NYPD's Juvenile Robbery Intervention Program, described in some detail in the chapter 'Gangs, guns and violence', are a perfect example. Proactive approaches before a young person turns 13 are urgently needed to prevent gang membership and a life of crime.

But isn't that true of all things? The best way to survive a car accident is to be vigilant and not get into one in the first place. And the best way to survive cancer is to catch it early when you can do something about it. The only programs that will have any long term impact on reducing our violent deaths are the ones which identify persons at-risk, those with a potential to commit suicide or youth exposed to gang membership, and take proactive efforts to reduce access to firearms.

Cure Violence makes the point that "On a larger-scale, the traditional approach to violence has been through a criminal justice lens focusing on prosecution over prevention. This framework views success in terms of clearance rates (those captured and incarcerated after the commission of a crime) and measures prevention through a crime-control perspective often termed in military language ("war on drugs," war on gangs"). Cure Violence looks to shift the discourse toward the view of violence as a disease and placing the emphasis on finding solutions to end this epidemic."

Obviously, they are on to something. As this problem costs all of us, it concerns all of us. And the previous back end focus on incarceration rather than prevention hasn't worked.

Cure Violence continues with the observation that, "Most of our program participants are beyond the reach of traditional social support systems. They have dropped out of school, exhausted social services or aged out, and many have never held a legitimate job; their next encounter with the system is either to be locked up behind bars or laid out in the emergency room. Our staff gets in where others can't, meets the participant where they are, works to change their behavior and connect them to resources that would otherwise be out of reach."

Speaking about Cure Violence, the Robert Wood Johnson Foundation says "By treating violence as a learned behavior that can be 'unlearned,' Cure Violence offers a solution to a problem that had been seen as unsolvable. It shows that violence doesn't have to be the accepted norm in the community, thus helping to reduce fear and stress that can have severely toxic effects on vulnerable populations."

When it comes to the high emotional costs paid by individuals so impacted by lives cut short, it is that very toxic combination of fear and stress that are the biggest costs to a society plagued by gun violence.

10.

Overall summation of the problem

The availability of guns is directly connected to the many violent deaths we experience in America each year. Let's be clear, guns are at the heart of it - over 80 percent of the murders and 55 percent of all the suicides in the US are committed with guns.

And it almost doesn't matter where the guns come from, all sources are culpable. It is the ready availability that is at issue. The point being, if they are available in Georgia then they'll wind up on a Baltimore street. Legal or illegal. We are really good at distribution in this country. So, what happens in one place affects what happens everywhere else. And, as we saw in some of the anecdotes, they can even affect events across time. A gun bought by one generation, can threaten another.

We humans are an imperfect and broken people, and all of us are liable to make bad choices at some point. Yet, at the worst moment in our lives, the availability of a gun only magnifies the chance of a fatal consequence. Like gasoline on a fire. Guns aren't the fire to be sure, but they make a bad situation worse.

This is no truer than in the case of suicide. The reasons 'why' people take their own lives are as diverse as our population and the solutions are as varied. But the 'how' people take their lives is known completely. If a potentially suicidal person has access to lethal means, it dramatically heightens their chance of a successful suicide. Several studies, including one from the Harvard University School of Public Health, have concluded "where there are more guns, there are more suicides". Therefore, as part of a comprehensive approach to suicide prevention, reducing access to guns is essential and will save lives.

The second biggest group at-risk is our young people, who are the principal victims of homicide. And yet, there is little empathy for the teenage gun victim in the inner city, especially if they are a minority and a gang member. But they should not so easily be condemned. Youth, after all, is not a crime but a period of transition. Youthful indiscretion, acting out, testing their limits and expressing themselves in non-verbal ways is guaranteed. Making sure they do these things in a safe environment without access to weapons improves the chances that those bad choices have no permanent or fatal consequences. And addressing the reasons young adults find solace in a gang rather than other means of belonging and economic opportunity must be a priority for us.

Certainly no sustainable society can permit so many youth at-risk of a violent death. And it is profoundly wasteful for us to spend so much after the crime, when that same money or less could be spent prior to the crime, through intervention rather than incarceration.

Clearly, what we've been doing, regarding homicide and suicide, hasn't been sufficient. A new mindset is long overdue. And controlling access to guns is at its core.

Section Two: Our misconceptions;

the myths and biases that hinder our debate

If one were to observe the recent debates on violence and guns in America, it would be easy to conclude that this book was addressing a wholly different country with quite different issues. There is an apparent disconnect between the problems as they are and the problems as outlined in most TV and newspaper coverage.

Unfortunately, it is the debates themselves that are too often focused on the wrong issues. Our ability to see this problem clearly has become impaired by certain myths and biases endemic to our culture. Too often, one hears discussions about guns in America using false myths to support a position. Yet, if we are to mitigate this major public health risk, our best chance is to have as clear and informed a discussion on these matters as is possible. The following section offers a review of some of the prevailing false myths in America and how they confuse our ability to really address this important matter. Hopefully, by identifying some of them, they will cease to be an impediment to our public conversation.

11.

The lone madman myth; the case of Sandy

Hook Elementary

Due in large part to the recent mass shootings – Columbine, the Colorado movie theater and Sandy Hook Elementary – the overall subject of guns and violence in America has gained far more notoriety and urgency than it had previously. In our complex and multi-issue world, it often takes a tragic and deadly incident to focus our attention on one problem over a myriad of other important matters. Certainly the flurry of news coverage and the rapid shift in public polls, following the Newtown massacres, has moved law makers of all stripes to respond.

In fact, it is usually easier on our representatives in doing their jobs if they receive a clear message from the public on what is expected of them. Hence state assemblies like New York's, which is famous for not working well, passed new gun control measures in a matter of weeks, even in a holiday season!

Unfortunately, the focus of all this activity has perhaps been too slanted toward the issue of the mentally unstable (the so called 'mad man with a gun'). Yet mass shootings don't represent the bulk of the problem.

If one were to add up the casualties to the three aforementioned events, the total deaths involve less than 50 persons. Terrible to be sure for all those involved, but a far cry from the tens of thousands of gun deaths which happen in the US each year. So why the focus on the lone madman? In part because it is such a classic fear, like the beast under the bed or the monster in the closet. And also in part because it causes politicians to dodge the real issues. It deflects us from the greater problem.

Let's look at the facts. According to the FBI 2010 study "*Crime in the US*", 78 percent of murders in the US were committed by someone with a relationship to the victim. And nearly one third (31.7 percent) of the homicides occurred between family members. The largest single causes of murders therefore are such things as arguments, brawls and gang activity – that is, neighborhood/family/workplace stuff. Felony types between strangers (rape, theft, burglaries) were only 23 percent. Assaults by strangers using guns is even less.

Therefore, the primary threat of murder comes from an argument or altercation with a known person (family, friend, neighbor, work associate), escalating into fatal violence due to the presence of a weapon. Violence from strangers with guns is an extremely rare incident indeed. While the lone madman with a gun is indeed terrifying, thankfully the incidents are rare and should not be allowed to cloud our vision of the bigger problem. If all we do is develop laws and policies aimed at Sandy Hook type incidents, we will have failed to address the bulk of firearm deaths in our country.

12.

The "guns make you safer" myth

One of the most profound differences in perception of gun ownership between gun owner and non gun owner is with the notion of safety; do guns in the home make one more safe, or less? We know from research that 67 percent of legal owners say they own guns for protection against crime, more than for sport or hunting, according to Gallup in a 2005 survey. In fact, 71 percent of gun owners think a gun in the house makes them more safe, compared with 23 percent of non-owners. And the indications from the urban youth seem to match; for those who have access to a gun, their primary reason to obtain a gun is also safety. It's also their primary reason to join a gang.

Are these two diverse groups assessing the situation correctly? The answer is no, the gun owners have it wrong. Consider some of the following supporting reports;

CNN in a January 2013 article state, "it's unclear whether the benefits of having a loaded and readily available gun in one's home outweigh the drawbacks. 'It's more common for an armed homeowner in the United States to be a victim of suicide, homicide, assault or an accidental shooting than it is for that person to shoot an intruder,' according to Dr. Arthur Kellermann, a senior health policy analyst at Rand Corporation, a non-partisan think tank. Kellermann led research for the Centers for Disease Control and Prevention in the 1990s which found that people who have guns in their homes are nearly three times more likely to be a victim of homicide and nearly five times more likely to commit suicide.

Experts also say that simply having a gun for self-protection does not guarantee safety."

According to *Bloomberg Businessweek* "In America, people who live in houses with guns are more likely to be killed. Homes with guns are 12 times more likely to have household members or guests killed or injured by the weapon than by an intruder"

According to TheHill.com, Rep. Henry Waxman (D-Calif.), the top Democrat on the Energy and Commerce Committee, wrote to Vice President Biden in early January 2013 recommending more research applying a public-health perspective to gun violence and greater mental health coverage for people in the United States. In his letter, Waxman urged attention to gun violence as an issue of public health, citing studies that show a "three-fold greater risk of homicide and a five-fold greater risk of suicide for residents in homes with firearms. Unfortunately," Waxman continued, "these research initiatives have been stymied by congressional funding direction and riders that have effectively shut down public health agencies … from conducting or sponsoring certain kinds of gun-related research."

Representative Waxman is referring to the Tiahrt Amendment, which Congress was persuaded to pass in 2003, which effectively blocks much of the data and research needed to get to the truth in the matter. According to the *Washington Post* in a 2010 article entitled 'Industry pressure hides gun traces, protects dealers from public scrutiny', "Under the law, investigators cannot reveal federal firearms tracing information that shows how often a dealer sells guns that end up seized in crimes. The law effectively shields retailers from lawsuits, academic study and public scrutiny. It also keeps the spotlight off the relationship between rogue gun dealers and the black market in firearms."

Surely, if we are to understand the problem, we need access to the data. No meaningful dialog can take place without focusing on the truth. The Tiahrt Amendment protects gun manufacturers and dealers by suppression of information. This is unacceptable. Who protects the citizens who are dying? If we did this with child seat safety data or research into the risks of second hand smoke, there would be an outcry. This is one really logical place to start – repeal the Tiahrt Amendment. In all our legislative efforts, the bias should be to favor the most defenseless and preserve life. Not commerce and hobby over life.

Mayors Against Illegal Guns (MAIG) is a coalition of over 800 mayors who support a number of gun control initiatives that the group calls "commonsense reforms" to fight illegal gun trafficking and gun violence in the United States. A priority goal of Mayors Against Illegal Guns is to repeal the Tiahrt Amendment. These are the people who are on the front line of gun violence. MAIG's web site states "These remaining Tiahrt restrictions keep the public, the media, academic researchers and elected officials in the dark about who gun traffickers are and how they operate. The Obama Administration should take the first step in repealing them by omitting them from its FY2014 budget. Congress should follow suit by affirmatively removing them from FY2014 appropriations bills."

Certainly repealing TIAHRT is a very good place to start. But regardless of its suppression of academic study, there is substantial evidence to indicate that the presence of a gun in the home increases the likelihood that someone in that home will be hurt by it. Even the Harvard Injury Control Research Center found significant evidence that more guns translates into more murders. This is true from rural to urban. And yet the myth persists, that guns increase safety, when the truth is quite the opposite. So how do we change minds? How do we dispel this most dangerous of myths?

13.

Ban assault weapons and everything will be

OK

For obvious reasons after the Sandy Hook Elementary shooting, a large part of the national discussion focused on assault weapons. And because they look so inappropriate for civilian use, having been designed for military purposes, the visual image of these things makes for good television. To be sure, it's hard to imagine why any human being needs these types of weapons that are meant to kill in high numbers. This cannot be justified by either sport or self defense and it is appalling that our Congress cannot even bring themselves to ban these weapons. One has to question the sanity of a system which allows the following person access to high capacity weapons.

Anecdote 10: the case of Alan Zaleski, Berlin, CT (compiled from US Department of Justice Press Release, February 3, 2011).

According to the evidence provided at trial, in 2005, a tree cutter contracted by a local utility company went to ZALESKI's heavily-wooded property in Berlin to cut back some trees from power lines and inadvertently tripped over one of several tripwires set up on the property, triggering a percussion explosive that detonated and caused him permanent hearing loss in one ear. When the utility worker returned to the property in August 2006 and noticed the tripwires again, he contacted the police.

Law enforcement officers responded and spent the next three days systematically searching ZALESKI's property, rendering many hazards safe, and seizing numerous weapons. During the course of the search, officers seized dozens of fully automatic machine guns and semi-automatic firearms, multiple rifles and handguns, as well as silencers, fragmentation grenades, chemical grenades, smoke grenades and various homemade pipe bombs and IEDs. ZALESKI also was found in possession of more than 67,000 rounds of live ammunition, and numerous components for making additional grenades, IEDs and bombs, including ammonium nitrate and nitro methane. Investigators also discovered that ZALESKI's property was protected by several booby traps, including tripwires connected to percussion explosives and camouflaged plywood boards on the ground with nails sticking up through them.

ZALESKI also possessed dozens of how-to books on making bombs and IEDs; converting semi-automatic weapons to fully automatic weapons; and making homemade silencers.

Law enforcement worked over a three-day period in August 2006 to seize more than 600 separate items of evidentiary value from ZALESKI's residence, one of the largest seizures of illegal weapons and other paraphernalia in state history.

On March 27, 2009, a jury found ZALESKI guilty of 28 counts related to the illegal possession of those firearms. In February, 2011, ZALESKI was sentenced by a Senior United States District Judge in New Haven to 101 months of imprisonment, followed by three years of supervised release, for illegally possessing machine guns and numerous other unregistered weapons, including a sawed-off shotgun, silencers, grenades and improvised explosive devices or "IEDs."

*   *   *   *

This story alone inspired me to name this book *Unsafe in Human Hands.* We have a little over six years to work on limiting access to these weapons, so that when Alan Zaleski gets out, he won't go gun shopping again.

But as horrific as the image of Zaleski's weapons cache is, and as devastating as assault rifles are for the victims of mass shootings, one has to ask – are they a statistically significant part of nationwide violent crime? And sadly, the answer is no. Estimates vary, but it's estimated that as low as 2 percent of violent crime in America is committed using assault style weapons. The frightening implications of this are, if we devote all our energies to banning assault weapons, then we are still left with the remaining 98 percent. Our energies need rebalancing to include other more common weapon types.

That doesn't mean the assault weapons don't represent a frightening trend in the marketing and production of guns. Fundamentally, manufacturers have a problem – a declining customer base. The percentage of households which report owning a gun, has been dropping for more than 30 years – down 40 percent according to the *General Social Survey*. This is a mighty head wind for any manufacturer to overcome. It's a little like being the last maker of VCR machines when no one is using them anymore. Your only option is to diversify.

So the gun manufacturers have added new products that would appeal to the normal gun owner, enticing him to buy more guns. And it's working. While the number of gun owners has reduced, these folks are buying more and more guns. It is a very specialized market with an estimated 20 percent of gun owners possessing 65 percent of the nation's guns (2007 Harvard University survey). This is partly why you see weapons originally designed for the military making it into people's homes. If your customer base for hand guns and rifles is shrinking, you need to find new product that appeal to this same market. You also need to find new markets, and that explains the recent efforts by gun manufactures to promote to women, with specialized gun clubs and custom designed guns in pink and other designer colors.

Each of these strategies could be found in any car or cola company's play book. In and of themselves, they are just standard marketing tactics for any American consumer product company. Not evil by any means, just business.

To illustrate these same market dynamics, one can see the same trend with military weapons manufacturers. The companies that supply our nation's military face declining customer demand too, only their customer base in a party of one. Consider the two examples of tanks and land mines.

The US bought an enormous number of tanks in the past decade for use in Iraq and Afghanistan, and as you can imagine, with our withdrawal, those orders are drying up. What do you do, if you run a tank manufacture, and your number one client is about to stop ordering? You need to replace that business. Says an IBISWorld Report on Tank and Armored Vehicle Manufacturing in the US, "While the US government will cut funding on tank and armored vehicle manufacturing, demand from foreign governments will help offset a major decline".

This also helps to explain why Belgian landmines end up in Libya. As a small country often overrun during Europe's many wars, Belgium made land mines for centuries. It was one of the world's largest producers. But with peace extending across post WWII Europe for the first time in recorded history, new markets had to be found. Peace, after all, is bad for weapons sales. So Afghanistan was filled with Belgian landmines as were Somalia, Iraq, Lebanon and Rwanda (the latter is one of Belgium's former colonies in Africa). Such a nice legacy to leave. Belgium, to its credit, has since signed the Ottawa Treaty with a goal to stop production, destroy stockpiles and to clear previously mined areas of all mines. And they say that Rwanda has since been cleared of all mines. But someone was selling rather than destroying stockpiles, and several of the old mines ended up in Libyan armories. Go figure.

This is the fundamental truth to marketing and distribution – if you are good, you will extend your products to all channels. If they exist anywhere, your products will exist everywhere. And that is true also of guns. If they exist on a ranch in Wyoming or a shooting range in Texas, they will also end up on a street in Baltimore or a remote home in the woods of Connecticut.

So what do we do about assault weapons? Certainly at only 2 percent of violent crime, even banning assault weapons completely wouldn't end violent deaths in present day America. But such a ban might have a big impact on our future. This concerted marketing effort by gun manufacturers to promote these products is bound to make assault weapons more prevalent in future and hence the importance of responding to this threat while it's still manageable.

14.

Racial barriers to empathy

It has been suggested by some that race defines why America was so moved by the shooting at Newtown, CT. However, I don't think it was race directly but rather age of the victims. It is easy to dismiss a teenage gang member's death as someone who had it coming, but one cannot do that with a 5 year old. By definition, a child is innocent. So we are forced to confront the horrible truth of that massacre. But there are so many other deaths from guns. How do we perceive those? And does race play a role in our perception of all gun users and the victims of homicide or suicide?

We know that race does play a large part in the American media's use of imagery. For example, if someone young is thought to have been abducted, it is usually the cute, white, blond girl who gets the most press coverage. Consider the recent cases of Natalie Holloway, Kayla Campbell, Elizabeth Smart, Caylee Anthony or Madeleine McCann.

But does race play into our ability to empathize with someone else? Do we see a dead person of another race in the same compassionate way we see someone from our own race? We do know that people's facial recognition or face perception drops dramatically outside of one's own race. However, this is dramatically altered with the more other-race experience you have – those with more other-race experience are consistently better at discriminating between other-race faces (Walker & Tanaka, 2003, Ekman & Friesen in 1976 and Ducci, Arcuri, Georgis & Sineshaw in 1982). But does this translate to empathy? Yes, empathy seems to also be affected by race.

In June 2012, an article in *Current Biology* entitled *Intergroup Empathy: How Does Race Affect Empathic Neural Responses?* states, "Recent neuroimaging evidence indicates that race modulates affective and cognitive components of empathic neural response. One recent neuroimaging study found that White and Asian participants show increased empathic neural response within the supplementary motor area, ACC, and lateral frontal cortices when perceiving a needle penetrating a same-race face, but decreased ACC response when perceiving a needle penetrating an other-race face. Another recent neuroimaging study showed that, for Black and White participants, empathy for ingroup members was neurally distinct from empathy for humankind more generally." The authors concluded, "The results of all of these studies indicate that empathic neural response is heightened for members of the same race, but not those of other races."

So, to humanize the stories of people faced with guns and violence in America, as this book is trying to do, we have a challenge; race plays a part in our ability to feel compassion about 'the other'. It also stands to reason that people cannot empathize as well with someone from a completely different culture and lifestyle. This may further compound our inability to understand each other, whether the person is a young man in the inner city if one has never lived in a city, or he is a rural white middle-aged male gun owner if you've never met such a person.

So much of this debate takes place on TV, which is visual, or through personal experience, which is also visual. In those circumstances, it is impossible to separate the human stories from the race of the participants. One of the hopes of this book is that race is not visually apparent in the anecdotes and therefore the human story might be perceived with more empathy and compassion. As Martin Luther King once said, "True compassion is more than flinging a coin to a beggar; it is not haphazard and superficial. It comes to see that an edifice which produces beggars needs restructuring."

Never has something needed more restructuring than the policies of gun ownership in America. And we will only do it if we can understand the suffering of others. Whatever role race plays in clouding our judgment, we must work against it to see the heart of the matter. We must resist any personal temptation to dismiss 'the other' as irrelevant to our daily lives. Our future as a country is inexorably bound up in each other's pathways with one future. "If one member suffers, all the members suffer with it . . ." (1 Corinthians 12:26).

15.

The changing American experience,

becoming two Americas

It becomes increasingly harder to set public policy when there are two different and distinct Americas emerging. One is mostly likely to be pro-gun and lives in rural or lower density population areas. And the other lives in urban centers, where gun ownership is viewed very differently. However, among the two lifestyles, it is the urban experience that is growing. In both the United States and the World, the move to urban centers seems an unstoppable trend. In 2007, for the first time in history, the UN estimates that the majority of people worldwide live in towns or cities. America's urbanization rate, having started in the Industrial Revolution, is even higher than most other countries and is increasing. It is becoming the norm of the American experience – most importantly for young people - and this represents vast changes in a society whose social compact was written in an agrarian age. These differences affect not only our Constitutional interpretation and application, but the demographic shifts which are dramatically affecting our recent politics and altering the mix of messages we send our representatives.

Yet, the profile of the legal gun owner is far from urban. In fact, although gun owners represent a divergent group, there are clear trends – they are far more likely to be male, white, rural, southern or midwestern, republican, a veteran, a protestant, and with no college degree. White voters are substantially more likely to own guns than Hispanics or blacks.

Since gun owners are two times more likely to live in rural environments than urban ones, the nature of human encounters in cities versus less densely populated places is an important distinction and can make a difference to our understanding of one another. For city dwellers, like your author, there is something physical in how we interact with our fellow citizens that makes our common urban experience quite different from other settings. Clearly anyone who visits a big city for the first time discovers with shock just how overbearing crowds and the constant press of humanity can be.

All the noises, the different languages, the smells. Streets are both fascinating places for people watching and certainly the architecture can be compelling. But they are also pungent places of ethnic food carts juxtaposed to bags of refuse, a passing lady's perfume one moment and the smell of urine the next. Get on a subway or bus and you are likely to be in personal physical contact with a half dozen strangers on a level of intimacy you hadn't ever planned on. Add to that; construction noises, ambulance sirens, beggars and street musicians, and the sensory input can be overwhelming if you're not used to it. For those who live in more rural places, it must seem like a level of hell to run away from.

And yet, cities are becoming the prevailing home place for our culture. The US is the most urbanized major country in the world (three quarters of the population of the United States live in density, and only one quarter in rural settings). In fact, more than half of all Americans live in the largest metropolitan areas, (populations of 1 million or more) partly because cities have more job opportunities. They offer young people more economic opportunities plus the cultural excitement they crave. As a distributor of resources, densely populated areas are also far more efficient, with huge infrastructure and public transportation. Commutes are therefore shorter. People drive less. Apartments even waste less heat than houses, with each unit only showing one outside wall to the elements. In all, there is a lot to argue for this kind of living.

As a result, we in the city have created a distinct society that differs from the rural experience. It is one of immediate encounter with "the other". Within a cul-de-sac, or gated community of like income and back grounded people, or tightly cocooned in one's car at the traffic light, one does not experience this direct connectivity with others. Yet, in a city, being human is a contact sport. It is very much an in-your-face experience.

Urban areas are also places of alternative lifestyles, including people who don't fit in elsewhere, for whatever reason. For example, I have been a single man for most of my life, and I've tried living in small towns, suburbs, mid size cities and mega cities. I was not easily accepted in small town culture. I know from personal experience, my life has been the fullest in mega cities like London and New York. I seem to fit in easily here.

There is another aspect to urban living. What is sometimes called "creative tension". All those highly motivated people trying to be the next big thing tend to push us all forward. I cannot begin to tell you how many people I know who have written books or are taking a break to write one. I know movie makers, TV actors, classical musicians, and people whose jobs I cannot even explain. I even have a friend who makes a living hosting her own radio show on BlogTalkRadio, describing herself as a creative vagabond and story teller (sandraleeschubert.com). My brother who lives in the horse country of South Jersey reports it's not like that. These highly specialized jobs, self made in new frontier industries, don't exist in every market in the US. It is but one example of the difference in our culture. It also explains these two America's from the human perspective and perhaps gives a tiny clue into the origins of our division on the gun issue. Maybe if both sides appear more human, we can communicate better. And find some resolution.

It is possible that those who live in rural areas far from this alien urban landscape feel some fear induced by its "otherness"? Perhaps they see the crime on TV and in movies, inducing them to buy guns for protection from something they don't understand and are afraid will someday show up on their doorstep to invade them (remember, safety is reported as the number one reason for buying a gun).

I don't always stay in the city. As I travel, people sometimes tell me how they feel like strangers in their own country. How many times have you heard someone say that going through Miami airport is like being in a foreign country? Yet for the residents of Miami, that is their American experience. How do we reconcile this? In New York City, 4 of 10 residents over the age of 5 speak a language other than English at home, and about 36 percent of all residents here are foreign-born. So which is the real America? Isn't each America as valid an experience as another? And how do these distinctly different Americas affect our understanding of one another? How do we learn to empathize with each other with our unique problems and perspectives? Or do we?   Can we find common ground?

A fine academic paper from the University of Stanford (Tobler's Law, Urbanization, and Electoral Bias - 2009) addresses one aspect of this – shared location.   They claim that " . . . voters are clustered into neighborhoods with other individuals who display similar attitudes and behavior (Key 1949, Taylor and Johnston 1979, Huckfeldt 1979, Johnston 1992, O'Loughlin 2002, Klos 2008, Cho and Gimpel 2009). Social scientists have developed a wide range of arguments about the possible causal mechanism behind such 'neighborhood effects,' but given the difficulty of empirical identification, there is little agreement about the independent causal role for social context beyond individual-level characteristics in explaining attitudes and behavior (Durlauf 2004). Yet as a descriptive fact, the spatial dependence of political behavior is widely observed in practice. The key implication of Tobler's Law for our purposes is that political behavior is spatially dependent: the probability that two voters exhibit similar political preferences or behavior is a function of the distance between their residential locations." Using Florida as their test case, they demonstrate the following conclusion; "We use detailed voting data from Florida to illuminate a pattern whereby urban centers are densely packed with leftists, while right-wing voters form more modest majorities in suburban and rural areas."

This is not just an isolated case in Florida. The same authors note "Preliminary analysis suggests that a similar pattern prevails in recent elections in much of the upper Midwest and Northeast, where Democrats are highly concentrated in dense, homogeneous cities, and Republicans maintain modest majorities in more heterogeneous suburbs, towns, and rural areas."

As we can see, this has implications in assessing our attitudes toward guns, both by party affiliation, but given the data just presented, really it's more by geographic place of residence. Something about our living together and sharing that experience coalesces into a unified viewpoint. And we couldn't be more diametrically opposed. According to the *General Social Survey*, gun ownership (the number of people with guns) has declined over the past 40 years, and yet almost all of the decrease has come from Democrats (urban settings, remember?). Despite their being more guns in America than ever before, by 2010, the gun ownership rate among adults that identified as Democrats had fallen to 22 percent, yet it remained at about 50 percent among Republican adults.

In so many ways, we are a more divided nation that at any time since the Civil War. We have different views on the role and size of government, the nature of job creation, America's place in the world, lifestyles, family structure and more. Our representatives reflect these divisions, which is largely why they can't come together any more than we can. In the absence of a clear message from us, they flounder.

And yet, when there is clarity, government works. Just a month after the Sandy Hook Elementary shooting, New York State passed the most stringent gun control laws in the nation. A state legislature famous for not working well managed to come together in remarkably short time and high resolve, to pass quick yet strong legislation. It was because the people of the state were speaking with one voice, and it empowered their leaders.

Appointing elected representatives is a little like hiring a house painter. You can check their previous work, but you don't leave them to select the colors of your house. You give them clear marching orders (yellow matt paint with green gloss shutters and white gloss trim). If you leave it up to their creative spirit, you might come home to find a purple house with wavy black stripes. Even a good house painter needs your input.

So too with our legislators. If we present them with mixed messages, our representatives simply mirror our own divisions.   If at all possible, we need some public consensus in this debate rather than wait for leadership to come from politicians. This is our job.

16.

Changing demographics are altering the

political power base

America has reached a tipping point. At some time during the past two years, the number of non-white births surpassed 50 percent. We are becoming a nation of minorities. This plurality will lead to cultural stress as an older, mostly white population grows increasingly estranged from the younger, mostly Latino, Black, and Asian new Americans. Sometimes called the "minority majority", there are three main groups – women, Latino and black – which are growing the most in political power. When it comes to the issue of gun ownership, they are united by a vested interest; women because it's their kids who are most at-risk, Latinos and blacks because they are far more likely to live in urban settings and view gun availability as a threat, not a source of safety.

The evidence that this is changing the political landscape was seen when the "minority majority" clearly cast the deciding vote in the last national election. According to Pew Data, the evidence of the demographic transformation of the electorate is seen in the profiles of each candidate's supporters: fully 89 percent of Romney's were white non-Hispanics, compared with just 56 percent of Obama's supporters. By contrast, Obama won 80 percent of non-white voters, the same as four years ago.

The pluses to this demographic shift are economic in nature and should be celebrated. Without the growth provided by these previously minor groups, our population would be static or in decline. In fact, across the industrial world, white populations are not replacing themselves. So to continue building a new work force plus consumers for our products, we need to find the growth someplace.

The downside is the source of fear it can provide some members of our population due to cultural alienation. Mark Potok, spokesman for the Southern Poverty Law Center (SPLC), which monitors hate groups says, "The demographic change in this country is the single most important driver in the growth of hate groups and extremist groups over the last few years." ABC News sites the SPLC as saying the number of radical "anti-government" militia groups increased from 150 to 1,274 during the years of the Obama presidency. "There have been more homegrown domestic terrorism attacks by right-wing groups than by international terrorists during his presidency as well", Potok noted.

Could this be the source of the fear which leads many gun owners to purchase weapons for self reported reasons of safety? Marilyn Mayo, co-director of the Anti-Defamation League's Center on Extremism, said, "It's a generalized feeling that 'this is not the country my Christian white forefathers built. We've got to take this country back.' It's not rancid straight ahead race hate, but it is very closely tied to race and the changing look of the country." Mark Potok summarizes my feelings exactly. "The thing I think to understand is that the radical right is not entirely composed of people who are insane. These are people reacting to real changes in the real world around them".

The good news is the youth in America show through the polls that they are much more comfortable with this transition than their elders. While this bodes well for the long term, it raises questions about the short term. Just like the questions raised in Section One regarding how we help young persons in the 15-24 age bracket transition safely into adulthood, there is a similar transition issue facing our broader population. As our demographic makeup changes, with cultural, political, and ideological changes following close behind, how do we shepherd our country through these shifts, bringing everyone along so no one feels left out? How can we avoid creating an increasingly smaller, disenfranchised group, militarily armed and hostile to the greater body of citizens? If the statistics are right that less and less people are buying more and more guns (gun ownership has fallen sharply from 54 percent of U.S. households in 1977 to 32 percent in 2011, according to the University of Chicago's *General Social Survey*), then this scenario doesn't end well if it's due to alienation and fear, armed to the teeth in preparation for war, and we do nothing to stop it.

Conclusion – the typical profile of the lawful gun owner represents a group descending demographically while on the other side the percentage of the population represented by the "minority majority" is rising and consequently their political power is rising too. This means both a political opportunity for some and an imperative for all.   It is a situation potentially rife with both good and bad aspects. It can give power to one side to make political change but risks from entrenching the other side - the remaining gun owners - in fearful and extremist positions. It is incumbent, therefore, to the anti-gun faction, to find an exit strategy if we as a nation are to make this transition peacefully. But it also implies that the Republican Party needs to face up to these demographic changes if they ever want to sit in power again since many of their positions, including gun ownership, appeal to a declining portion of the population.

17.

Civil religion – the branding of the American

myth

No country has been better at mythologizing its origins than the United States. In part it is because we are so young compared to the Old World and therefore out origins lie within the timeframe of recorded history. We even have original source documents. By contrast, the origins of China, India and Egypt are shrouded in legends. Their nations were not created out of whole cloth but rather evolved into being like our species itself. As a consequence, they do not have an ideal against which they were forged. We are unique, therefore, among the great nations in that we were founded intentionally and have the added advantage of a narrative which, on the face of it, seems to be real and verifiable.

Out of these origins, we have created what is known as a civil religion – the deifying of our origin story. And like most religions, it has ideological aspects and sacred cows nobody wants trampled on. We have our hymns (America the Beautiful, Battle Hymn of the Republic), our saints (the Founding Fathers, Lincoln and Martin Luther King), our martyrs (war dead and those who died on 9/11) and our scriptures (Declaration of Independence and the Constitution). We even have our feast days (4th of July and Thanksgiving). We have built it into a world class religion. You can see it more easily when you go abroad and observe how often we "preach" this religion to others, especially around election time. It can, in fact, become quite annoying to others.

Certainly there are many positive qualities to a civil religion. It is, for us, the one unifying religion in a country which cannot agree on any other religion. Even if some say our country is predominantly Christian, the countless denominations we have today attest to the fact that even we Christians cannot come to an agreement on our one faith. So our civil religion serves as a unifying force in American life. It helps to give us a common set of values and identity when all other aspects of our lives are so profoundly different.

But there is a downside to civil religion, unfortunately, and that is when the mythology deviates too much from the reality. To be sure, we are unique in our belief in a steadfast defense of liberties, even among peoples in other parts of the world who are not Americans. "Justice is indivisible. Injustice anywhere is a threat to justice everywhere. And wherever I see injustice, I'm going to take a stand against it whether it's in Mississippi or in Vietnam," said Martin Luther King in 1967. Noble words. However, we know that justice, even in our own country, is unevenly applied. Dr. King himself was not praising American policy but protesting it, in the case of the Vietnam War, as being beneath our lofty national ideals. Even today, there is a gapping chasm between our ideal portrayed in our mythology and the everyday reality which falls far short. We might tell ourselves that we defend liberties wherever they are threatened, but too often we only act on that precept when our self interests are involved – like in oil bearing countries. And we don't always put ourselves at-risk in the defense of liberties, preferring too often to bomb from 30,000 feet or with unmanned drones.

Whether it is the Universal Church, our Nation, our families or our individual selves, it is normal to fall short of our ideals. It is only important that we be honest with ourselves as to where the truth lies, in order to close the gap and become the church, country or people that we want to be. Varnishing the truth doesn't help solve anything.

Therefore, I would like to demystify some of our origin myths with the intent of showing how they affect our ability to see the current debate on guns. The romantic image of the Minuteman with a musket over the mantle, ready to race to the defense of liberty against the armies of King George, is perhaps one of our most prevalent and yet unhelpful myths. It is often quoted as one reason why guns are part of our legacy. But that really isn't the reason. Our nation was not founded fresh out of the womb in 1776, but rather was nurtured and midwived into existence over a century and a half prior to the Revolution.

The path to a culture at arms is a long one, perhaps even rooted in a violent medieval Europe. But to understand how it transferred to the new world, and how it continued so much longer in America than in the Old World, one must go back to the beginning of European settlements in this country. And here is where it gets personal for me, because I have so many ancestors who were present in the Indian Wars of New England during 1620-1677. Some of my ancestors came on the Mayflower in 1620. In fact, the majority of my bloodline was already here by 1634, all arriving in New England. As they say, I have skin in this game.

Therefore, let us turn back the clock and take a look at a formative period in our past and evaluate the actual persons as contrasted with the myth.

Anecdote 11: Seventeenth Century New England

Before their landing, the Pilgrims wrote and signed something called the Mayflower Compact. It was a social contract itemizing their rights but also their duties and obligations each colonist should expect from one another. It had the very principle of founding a society in one single document, to bind them as well as empower them. Ten years later, Governor Winthrop who founded the

Massachusetts Bay Colony would elevate their calling by saying, " . . . for wee must Consider that wee shall be as a Citty upon a Hill, the eies of all people are uppon us; soe that if wee shall deale falsely with our god in this worke wee have undertaken and soe cause him to withdrawe his present help from us, wee shall be made a story and a byword through the world . . . "

But with all their attention to each other, to the eyes of the world and to God, how did they fare in their treatment with the native peoples already living in these new lands?

First Encounter 1620

Certainly, the earliest settlers from Jamestown to Plymouth Rock had an uneasy first contact with the Native Americans. Different ideas on land ownership, problems with English livestock eating Indian food supplies, endless cultural differences and assumptions, rivalries between the various native tribes themselves, pressures from disease brought by the settlers, limited resources for growing populations all combined with a general sense of manifest destiny by the Europeans, led to fights over territory and power. From the beginning, conflicts between Indian groups were also aggravated by one tribe allying itself to the better armed Europeans for advantage over another tribe. Fighting was frequent, and with the colonists' back to the wall (read sea), with no option but to fight, someone was going to annihilate the other.

In what is known as the First Encounter with Native Americans, while the Pilgrims were still holed up in the Mayflower off shore during their first winter, a landing party came ashore to scout for a possible settlement site and to obtain supplies (i.e. stealing corn from Indian supplies). Led by Myles Standish, and including my ancestor Richard Warren, a small group made several forages onto Cape Cod until, on December 8, 1620, they were attacked by Indians. The two groups exchanged arrows and musket fire, the pilgrims losing not a man but at least one native was shot in the arm. It is impossible to know if he survived the wounding, but a musket ball, being handmade and irregular, spirals and tumbles in its trajectory, smashing into the victim leaving a large wound hard to clean. The event left the Indians bloodied and the Pilgrims fearful. From then on, their exploration was further north in what became Plymouth Colony.

The first non-violent relationship took place the following spring and involved a treaty with Massasoit, Chief of the Wampanoag tribe, using the translation services of Squanto who had learned English before the Pilgrims ever left England. In the increasing conflicts between the Wampanoag (Massasoit's tribe) and the Narragansett (Massasoit's domestic rivals), Massasoit sought a treaty made between him and the English for mutual protection. Given the Pilgrim's earlier experience at First Encounter, they jumped at the chance. From the Indian perspective, as Governor Winslow later said in his diaries, "because hee [Massasoit] hath a potent Adversary the [Narragansetts], that are at warre with him, against whom hee thinkes wee may be some strength to him…".

Pequot War 1637-1638

One clear example of European and domestic American politics colliding in early New England involved the areas between what we now call the Connecticut and Hudson Rivers. In the 17th Century, this was disputed land between the Dutch colonies of New Holland (now New York) and the English colonies in New England. Ironically, this particular border dispute didn't get fully resolved until after the American Revolution (when my ancestors moved from the Massachusetts coast to Hillsdale, NY, in 1785, it is possible they believed they were still in Massachusetts!).

It didn't help that the Pequot Indians and their allies the Mohegans lived right in the middle of this European turf war, and in addition were themselves want to fight other Indians over land rights having already brutally displaced the previous native inhabitants several generations before. In 1630, making challenges against everyone on their borders, the Pequot committed numerous violent acts upon the English, the Dutch and the Narragansett Indians. Things were coming to a head for everybody. By 1631, it got more complex. Having formerly acted as a single group, the Pequot divided in two factions; pro-English and pro-Dutch. This led to a protracted set of battles and skirmishes, complex alliances, betrayals, and finally a massacre of the pro-Dutch faction by the English settlers. Alden T. Vaughan wrote in his book New England Frontier: Puritans and Indians 1620-1675: "The effect of the Pequot War was profound. Overnight the balance of power had shifted from the populous but unorganized natives to the English colonies. Henceforth (or until King Philip's War 40 years later) there was no combination of Indian tribes that could seriously threaten the English. The destruction of the Pequots cleared away the only major obstacle to Puritan expansion. And the thoroughness of that destruction made a deep impression on the other tribes." After the war, the Pequot people were dispersed as chattel among the other tribes, the Pequot lands were given over to the Connecticut Colony (much to the disputation of the Dutch), but at least a kind of peace existed for more than a generation.

King Philip's War 1675-1677

The next chapter from New England's perspective was King Philip's War (so named for the Indian Chief who led the rebellion, known by the English as Philip). It was now 1675, and New England had changed considerably in only two generations. Just 150 persons arrived with the Mayflower in 1620, half of whom died by the first spring, and in 1630, Governor Winthrop had brought another 700 persons to Massachusetts, 200 of whom died in the first year. Tiny numbers indeed. Yet by the time of King Philip's War, the

English population had swelled to at least 60,000 people, putting enormous pressure on land, water resources and hunting space. By contrast, the Native population had been dwindling even before the Mayflower. The passing English trading ships who had visited the region even before 1620 had introduced small pox and viral hepatitis epidemics, and some of the tribes were already under stress at the time of the Pilgrims arrival. (This pattern mimicked what the Spanish experienced in Central and South America, finding whole parts of the interior depopulated by disease before they even arrived).

The native population in New England had always lived mostly by hunting and fishing. Yet considerable amounts of their ancestral land had been taken or bought by the English settlers and ironically, the Indians had coped with these loses, by being able to catch more in less space through the prevalent use of firearms. By the time of King Philip's War, the native population used guns almost wholly for hunting (Soldiers in King Philip's War, George Bodge). Bodge indicates that they were expert in the use of such firearms and considered them their most precious possessions. Yet, increasingly, the English were demanding that the Indians surrender these arms both in payment against breach of English laws and a general discomfort with so many armed natives. All these factors, and probably more, led them to rebellion.

The irony was, Philip was Massasoit's son. The very first Chief who had befriended the English for common cause against his enemies, was to be followed by a son who made war on the same English for his very survival – only to accelerate the end of his people, not save them.

The cost of the war in blood was high. My own kinsman, one Captain Isaac Johnson, was in command of a company of 75 and died leading the assault on the Narragansett fort in modern day South Kingstown, Rhode Island. Numbers are only speculative after so much time, but it is thought that close to three thousand Native Americans died during the entire 2 year conflict – nearly a third of their remaining New England population. A number of those who survived the war were later enslaved and deported to Bermuda. The English population had also lost thousands of adult men of productive working and breeding age. A huge portion of the region's economy and its towns and farm lands were in ruins, and rebuilding took years. The war created debts on New Englanders who had to repay Britain for its assistance. All this fighting took a terrible toll.

*   *   *

The role of taming the frontier and its part in creating the gun culture in contemporary America

So why are these colonial stories in a book about modern day violence and guns? Why have I devoted so much detail to a few points in history so long ago and why is it pertinent to our present predicament? In part, it is a personal exploration of a time when many of my ancestors lived and participated in the events of the day. I've always had a fascination with what motivated them to live their lives the way they did. Not that I would have wanted to be there. I suspect I wouldn't have related to them very much. My own Episcopal (Anglican) brand of worship was banned by 17th Century puritans in New England as it was by the Dutch in New Amsterdam. Christmas was outlawed as heathen revelry, papist and not supported by Holy Scripture. All this was bathed in a sense of manifest destiny – the notion that God had in some way given them this land, like the biblical land of Canaan, whose conquest by the Israelites begins at the battle of Jericho. As John Quincy Adams would later write, stopping western expansion was unsupportable simply "for the sake of preserving a perpetual desert for savages".

Here is what God said to the Israelites. "Now then, you and all these people, get ready to cross the Jordan River into the land I am about to give to them—to the Israelites. I will give you every place where you set your foot, as I promised Moses. Your territory will extend from the desert to Lebanon, and from the great river, the Euphrates—all the

Hittite country—to the Mediterranean Sea in the west. No one will be able to stand against you all the days of your life." Joshua 1:2-5

These first Europeans believed they had been given this land, having been chosen by God, like the Israelites. Unfortunately, this form of scriptural interpretation and application in the New World justified all manner of insult against the native population. From the First Encounter - when Myles Standish (and my own ancestor Richard Warren) set foot on New England soil in 18 December, 1620 – Indians and Puritans were shooting at one another and my ancestors were stealing Indian food supplies. Violence from day one. And it continued until their civilization lost and that of my ancestors won. No compromise.

I make no comment here on God and his covenants with Israel. Only the application of those covenants to the Puritans arriving in America. The Massachusetts Bay Colony considered its land claim to extend all the way to the Pacific. And it considered its right to the land a holy right and their conversion of the locals a holy cause. Anyone not Puritan wasn't really a true Christian either. It was, at a minimum, an intolerant era, and one we would hardly recognize.

Violence at our doorsteps

From their very first steps on land to the last big New England Indian War, it had been a fight. And this pattern was to continue across the continent as frontier after frontier opened up and then fell to development. Our foundational experience as Americans was confrontational, with violence at our very doorsteps. We fight wars today in distant countries, but in our formative years, violence was in our streets. In 17th Century New England, there were even laws requiring men to come to church armed, so dangerous was the possibility of Indian attack whenever that many people were gathered in one place, it was considered essential to be prepared.

There were three very broadly defined stages to this changing frontier (what I consider on-your-doorstep type of violence) in American history:

- The Indian Wars of New England followed by the French and Indian Wars on the edges of New England culminating in the Revolution.
- The control and suppression of slaves, the perceived or real threat of their possible revolt, the ensuing Fugitive Slave Act of 1850 and ultimately the Civil War.
- The Mexican American War and Western expansion into new territories with a new frontier made up of new native peoples.

I will spare the reader all the details of each, since books have been written on these subjects for the reader to explore at another time. But I will summarize what are some common elements of each and their application to our present time. Like the summary of the Indian Wars of New England, each of these broad phases were characterized by ever present violence, with both real and perceived threats, right in our streets and back yards. These were not distant wars fought "over there".

And all this happened before we had the powerful centralized government we have today to intercede. Fighting was done on a local level by local militia. And both sides of any fight used similar types of weaponry. An utterly different set of circumstances to our present world.

As each of these frontiers receded, starting in the Northeast, then the South, then the West, the social structure and indeed the perception toward violence changed dramatically. By the late 1800's, when Americans were still fighting natives in the West, in the Northeast, crime and violence were relegated to gangs and organized crime from a New

American population. It was already becoming two Americas.

The personal experience and lifestyle of the average resident in 1850 Boston as compared to say 1850 Utah could not have been more different. Back East, guns had already dissipated from the everyday experience of most citizenry.   Out West, guns played a different role, although not always because of the lawlessness Hollywood portrays, but because of the struggle with the native population. The interchange between the new Americans on the Western frontier it turns out was relatively peaceful. Despite the myth of Western lore, the so called Wild West was not any wilder than our society today and violence was restricted to conflicts with native persons. (Anderson, Terry, and P. J. Hill. 1979. An American Experiment in Anarcho-capitalism: The Not So Wild, Wild West.)

So far had the daily use of guns by law abiding citizens departed from the North's experience, it has been noted by many that gun marksmanship during the Civil War was appallingly bad. The very founding reason for the NRA, according to their own history, states "Dismayed by the lack of marksmanship shown by their troops [New York Regiment], Union veterans Col. William C. Church and Gen. George Wingate formed the National Rifle Association in 1871." William K. Emerson, writing in his book Marksmanship in the U.S. Army, says "hunting for food, served as the sole weapons training at many western posts. Troops 'back East,' without the freedom to hunt and lacking wild animals prowling around, had no such opportunity." He reports, "Some of the [Civil War] soldiers fired their muskets for the first time during battle."

These changes play very much into our perceptions of violence today. We have a huge gap to fill between our myths and our realities. The formative era of violence in America, was not so much the noble militiaman defending his liberties against foreign powers (British or Mexican or French), but the invasion of one people against another by force using a sense of superiority and religion as justification. Where one falls on the issue of gun control usually depends on how one views the above statement.

With the three broad frontier conditions no longer present – Indians lost the war totally, the slaves were freed and Mexico couldn't possibly take its land back – then what frontier threats were left to worry about? If the number one reason reported by legal gun owners for buying their guns is personal safety, then just who are they afraid of? Do we really think that America will return to a time when we need to take our guns to church to defend against Indians on the ride home?

If, at the core of gun ownership is a root fear, then we need to understand this fear. Given the change in America's experience over the past 400 years, I cannot see the condition of my colonial ancestors being relevant in my time; hence I don't own a gun. And I'm not alone. If one looks today at New England, the Mid-Atlantic States and the Industrial Midwest, which were the first regions of the country to push back their frontier conditions and also the states that never had significant slave populations, those regions are in fact the least likely today to report the presence of a gun in their home. It seems as the threats receded, so did the need for guns. And the ideologies changed too.

As a friend of mine from the Caribbean said, "why is there still a need for guns when the slaves aren't around to revolt anymore". If that was the fear, real or imagined, and circumstances changed, then why the continued presence of guns?

One fear suggested by some is that the government is going to come and take away their guns. That seems like circular logic; you buy a gun to make sure no one takes it away, a problem that wouldn't exist if you didn't buy the gun in the first place. Like taking a pill that prevents your need to take pills. Or beating your head against the wall, because it feels so good when you stop. Circular logic would be a sad reason for the existence of so many weapons.

I has also been suggested that gun manufacturers have militarized the guns they promote to make up for decreasing sales. We know that the number of gun owners in America is dropping, and that gun unit sales have not kept up with population growth. But with more sales to fewer and fewer gun owners, the result is each owner is buying an increasing number of guns. They must be motivated by something.

It is proposed by some that gun ownership is a check and balance against a tyrannical government. That might have been true during the revolution or even during the French & Indian wars. Or from the southerner's perspective during the "war of northern aggression". But not now. More often in modern times, the US is the aggressor abroad. Our military strategy for some time has been to meet the enemy on their home ground, long before they reach us here (take the war to the enemy).   So the only possible tyrannical government one might be afraid of is our own. Although we may disagree with our government sometimes, this conclusion is hard to swallow.

Yet, something is taking place that we need to understand. We know from the data that this minority are buying guns largely for safety, so some deep seated fear is at play. If we don't try to understand the fear which is underlying much of gun ownership, we risk creating an increasingly entrenched minority who are hostile to the rest of our society – never a good situation especially when heavily armed. One only has to consider our law enforcement personnel who would have to go up against those guns to see how we can never let that happen.

Getting inside people's heads may be the key to bringing us back from the edge. So far, the present legal action to control guns seems to only inflate the fear, not resolve it. We can't bring together two disparate groups by intimidation – even if one side has the legislative advantage to enforce their will – not if we want long term resolution.

In summary, the circumstances of our nation's formation may have been what led us to so much gun ownership, but those circumstances have fundamentally changed. Yet the culture remains. A legacy we can and ought to change. After all, look how much our views on smoking and divorce have changed in just a lifetime. Pervasive cultural viewpoints are not immutable. Hopefully, we can achieve a new mindset through persuasion rather than violence.

18.

The Second Amendment and the balance

between rights and obligations

Remarkably, the United States went from one of the youngest governments on Earth at our founding to one of the oldest today. So turbulent have the last two centuries been, that nearly every other government has seen a complete change in its structures except ours. World maps have been re-crafted and whole political systems have vanished as millennia old monarchies fell through revolutions. New ideologies, like fascism and communism, have come and gone. And still there is the government invented in that summer long ago in Philadelphia. Ironically, it hasn't been replicated in form successfully anywhere – Parliament, actually, is the most copied form of government on earth. But it has worked for us. And therein lies an important point; no one should dismiss such a successful political experiment lightly.

Yet, the glorious intent of our founders was not immediately implemented. Even when it was first presented, the Constitution was rejected by many. In the preamble to the Bill of Rights, it states "THE Conventions of a number of the States, having at the time of their adopting the Constitution, expressed a desire, in order to prevent misconstruction or abuse of its powers, that further declaratory and restrictive clauses should be added: And as extending the ground of public confidence in the Government, will best ensure the beneficent ends of its institution." So, the Constitution was altered to make up for perceived inadequacies. This process hasn't stopped. Our founding documents – the Declaration of Independence, the Constitution and the Bill of Rights - and the lofty ideals that were behind their formation - are still being realized.

For example, the notion that "all men are created equal" actually applied at first only to rich, white, male landowners. It took a lot of struggle over a very long time to extend that right to poor tenant farmers, women, blacks and – well – we're still working on gays and immigrants. And the notion that governments derive "their just powers from the consent of the governed" obviously didn't apply yet to the nearly 700,000 slaves who resided in the United States at the time the Constitution was written. Slave populations would swell to four million before anything one might call their consent would even be possible.

In fact, the notion of consent by all of us was different from how we see it today. Our government was founded as a republic (which only indicates a non-monarchy), but not quite the pure democracy as we now think of it. Thomas Jefferson once said, "A democracy is nothing more than mob rule, where fifty-one percent of the people may take away the rights of the other forty-nine."

Examples of our less than democratic beginnings abound. It was only 100 years ago this spring, for example, that the 17th Amendment forced the direct election of United States Senators by popular vote. Prior to that, Senators were appointed by State Legislatures, not by the people. And we know that, even today, the President and Vice President are not elected directly by the voters, but through a mechanism called the Electoral College which was a compromise since the original intent at the Constitutional Convention was to have Congress elect the President. We the people, it seems, were not a direct party to these methods. After all, how do you accommodate so many slaves who can't really be counted equally when apportioning seats in Congress?

Remarkably, our original form of government also did not take into account political parties, which did not yet exist and something Washington was firmly against. In its original form, the person with the most electoral votes became President, and the candidate receiving the second most votes would become Vice President. If this process were still followed today we'd have Romney working beside Obama!

There are many aspects of these original documents which are either observed in the breach or have been adapted to meet changing values and understandings of what a democracy entails. This is why the Supreme Court has morphed into a body which helps us to interpret the Constitution by reviewing the constitutionality of any law or judicial proceeding. Interestingly, the Constitution does not spell out this specific function – another observation in the breach – and judicial review has only been inferred and become common practice over time.

Therefore, as remarkable as our form of government is, its greatest strength, like a good skyscraper, is in its flexibility. From the very first, we kept correcting and adapting to change our understanding of this great experiment. So how does that help us today?

As it applies to the ownership of guns, the Second Amendment is often cited as foundational. "A well regulated militia being necessary to the security of a free state, the right of the people to keep and bear arms, shall not be infringed."

Now it has been suggested by some that the key to interpreting this amendment has been the first phrase's point about a militia and that personal guns outside of a functioning member of a people's militia was never intended. The Supreme Court has disagreed with that assertion in *District of Columbia v. Heller*, 554 U.S. 570 (2008) where they assert the public's right to possess a firearm independent of any membership in an organized militia. Therefore, I will not address this point, as I consider it answered. As a religious man, I'm also not a fan of nit picking over the letter of the law, rather than considering the spirit of the law.

My comments are reserved to the broader notion that liberties should and rightfully be balanced in proportion to the rights of others. As Thomas Jefferson pointed out, "rightful liberty is unobstructed action according to our will within limits drawn around us by the equal rights of others." He once described himself as "a warm zealot for the attainment and enjoyment by all mankind of as much liberty as each may exercise without injury to the equal liberty of his fellow citizens". And this is the point, isn't it? That one's right to bear arms must be weighed against the increased danger those guns cause to the residents of the household in which they reside. And further, the distribution of arms because of the laws of manufacturing and distribution means that access to lawfully purchased guns to some will guarantee the ready availability of those same type arms to others who should probably not have them at all, particularly our youth.

When the actions of some threaten the life and liberties of others, we turn to the natural and moral hierarchy within our many liberties to adjudicate. All rights, after all, are relative and some liberties take a subordinate position to others. In all cases, there is a balance between my rights and your rights; that is my liberties cannot impinge upon your liberties. Therefore, as the classic example goes, I cannot yell "fire" in a movie theater, because my right to free speech doesn't give me the right to endanger the lives of others during an unnecessary and panic filled exodus from a movie house. My right to free speech is subordinate to their right to live.

In all of these balancing of priorities, the preeminent liberty is always life. Yet, as we can see from all the credible research, the presence of a weapon in a house actually puts people's lives in danger. The residents of any house with a gun is at dramatically more risk that they will become victims of those very guns, either through homicide or suicide. So the predominate purpose of obtaining weapons for safety actually achieves the opposite. These weapons cause more suffering and loss of life than they provide any positive benefit, and so, gun rights should take a subordinate position to life rights.

Does this mean that guns cannot exist at all? No. But limitations on guns are both right and appropriate for any society in order to provide a safe environment for its citizens and especially its youth. So what would those look like? Let us take two common examples in everyday life.

Two activities that have long been enjoyed together are drinking and smoking. However, while our attempts to ban the former were disastrous, our limitations on the latter have been more successful. Why? This is in large part due to the public's tacit understanding that drinking poses dangers only to the user whereas smoking also produces dangers to those around the smoker through second hand smoke. So our laws limiting drinking apply only to minors. But our laws regarding the enjoyment and practice of smoking have become far more rigorous and constraining. Even the prevailing cultural attitudes to smoking have changed dramatically. Just look at an old black and white movie to see how we have changed our mindset. The principle here is, smoking is dangerous not just to the smoker but others around them, and therefore becomes subordinate to the public's right to good health.

Unlike drinking and smoking, another dangerous active that we all partake in – driving – is a necessity. For better or worse, we have built our modern society around cars and we require their services to work, shop and live our lives. Yet automobiles kill over 35,000 people a year! So our solution is to work on traffic safety, because banning automobiles is not a possibility. Yes, in the long run, because of urbanization, we could move a larger portion of our population into public transportation and alternative transportation. But in the short run, people live where they live and cars are indispensible. So increasing safety through consumer education programs and engineering advances have become the only avenues available to us. If, like cigarettes, we could ban their use in public, we would save more lives. But our country's infrastructure and economy could not accommodate the change, so we don't go that route.

Clearly, of the examples above, gun ownership more closely matches the profile of smoking than to drinking or cars. First, gun ownership is not the necessity that cars are.

One might challenge this by asking; doesn't the Second Amendment refer to "a well regulated militia being necessary to the security of a free state"? But the original principle of a free militia, being interpreted by the Supreme Court as a "militia comprised of all males physically capable of acting in concert for the common defense", already exists. We have this in the National Guard, and personal guns are not required. But should our government turn tyrannical and become a threat to the liberties of its people? The suggestion that an armed public could defend against a concerted effort by the American military is ludicrous. Entire alliances of nations have made war on the US unsuccessfully. A few armed individuals, even with automatic weapons, would pose more of a public threat than a benefit to freedom. The best defense against tyranny in modern times is an educated electorate. Washington said, "Promote then, as an object of primary importance, institutions for the general diffusion of knowledge. In proportion as the structure of a government gives force to public opinion, it is essential that public opinion should be enlightened." "Enlighten the people generally", Jefferson added, "and tyranny and oppressions of body and mind will vanish like evil spirits at the dawn of day."

One might also ask, aren't guns necessary for personal defense in the home? The Supreme Court has interpreted the Second Amendment as protecting an individual right to possess a firearm unconnected with service in a militia, and to use that arm for traditionally lawful purposes, such as self-defense within the home. In fact, it has endorsed the role of firearms when "the importance of the lawful defense of self, family, and property is most acute". However, it has also stated this right is not unlimited. It is not a right to keep and carry any weapon whatsoever in any manner whatsoever and for whatever.

Back to the comparisons with cars, drinking and smoking, the possession of guns, unlike drinking, poses a definite danger to those around them. More like secondary smoke, guns can cause lethal consequences to others. Therefore, the public is increasingly open to their limitations for the sake of public health and consequently gun legislation is both right and necessary to define limits.

So, yes, we have a right to bear arms, but within limits. And we have an established hierarchy of rights, with life itself to be preeminent above all others. Therefore, as a secondary right, gun ownership must be the one to accommodate.

19.

Is compromise possible?

In my introduction, I stated that America needs a change in mindset. But is that even possible? Happily, America has changed its mindset on many occasions before. In the early 60's, divorce made one a neighborhood pariah. Yet today, it's become so common place as to barely be worth mentioning. And our thoughts on smoking have changed dramatically through education and behavioral shifts. Just look at any old black & white movie, with men wearing coats and ties to baseball games (women are almost never present in those stadiums), and the omnipresence of public smoking is a shock to us modern types. In less than a lifetime, we have shown dramatic change in our tendency to affiliate with any one religious denomination and overall church attendance is down. We have broadly come to accept intercultural and interracial marriages without a second glance. And we're working on accepting homosexuality – our latest change in mindset.

These changes occur even in our own homes, where we've gone from formal dining rooms to casual great rooms; no longer do brides register sterling silver patterns or china – they are more likely to want a flat screen TV!

Our biggest cultural shift can be found in our attitudes toward women and blacks and the realization that the tyranny of the majority is as dangerous as tyrants were to our ancestors. So great have these changes been that we cannot even conceive of certain historical norms like white only bathrooms or male-only private clubs.

Yet each of these cultural shifts came only after concerted struggles by a few committed persons working ceaselessly until their ideas became accepted by the majority. In all such battles, false assumptions, cultural myths and biases, and general misinformation, were a challenge to good public discourse and policy. And as we have seen, the gun debate is no exception. But we should take heart – they are all things we can change. And so it is in the case of violence and guns, that none of this is unsolvable. A heightened awareness of the risks of gun ownership and the nature behind at-risk behavior of both young adults and persons with suicidal tendencies can go a long way toward reducing the many Americans we lose unnecessarily each year to violent deaths. It is one of the ways this book tries to contribute to the conversation.

The promise and costs of compromise

As we've seen, the rising demographics of the "minority majority" give that group the numerical advantage to enforce political change on others. Sadly, if not done correctly, this simply becomes another case of tyranny by the majority. As Alexis de Tocqueville, warned in his *Democracy in America*, "If ever the free institutions of America are destroyed, that event may be attributed to the omnipotence of the majority, which may at some future time urge the minorities to desperation and oblige them to have recourse to physical force. Anarchy will then be the result, but it will have been brought about by despotism." So how do we influence change without using despotic tyranny against an armed minority? Is some kind of compromise possible? This to me seems like a very urgent and important question at this crossroads.

Normally, I'm one for compromise. Some of the best decisions I've been associated with were when everyone won a little (or lost a little) and they all went away feeling equally treated. History is replete with unsettled scores when one side won a lopsided victory, inevitably guaranteeing a rematch. Nature, it seems, abhors an imbalance, and will seek equilibrium's return. As this is so important in the current political climate, I'd like to review at length two examples of compromise (one successful and one failure) and then relate how I think we should apply them to our current circumstances.

Anecdote 12: Germany between the wars.

The most famous example of unsettled scores can be found in Germany between the First and Second World Wars. Humiliated and bled by reparations after the First World War, resentment among the German speaking populations simmered. The haughty behavior of Europe's victors didn't help. This was the classic lopsided victory waiting for a rematch.

Pierrepont B. Noyes, a successful business leader at the time, was drafted as a delegate to the Paris Peace Conference by President Wilson and later was appointed to the American post in the commission which ruled Germany after the First World War.

At the Paris Peace Talks, Noyes observed that all the parties were devoting themselves not for mutual gain or a stable and peaceful Europe, but were in reality prepositioning themselves to be ready for the next war. As early as 1921, he began to predict the coming of another World War.

Noyes took great efforts to warn everyone including specifically telling President Wilson the Peace Talks would fail. So strongly did he feel about the coming of another war that he spent an entire year traveling about the United States making speeches in which he emphasized the danger inherent in Europe.

Sadly, we know how that turned out. As a consequence of these failures, and the awful costs of another war, the Allied powers vowed to do better next time. Two moments in particular stand out. At the beginning of the Second World

War, the then big two – Churchill and Roosevelt – agreed there would be no land gains as a result of the war, only a return to law and order (see Atlantic Charter, August 1941). It was an incredible set of limitations for two empires to impose upon themselves. Second, at the end of the war, the Marshall Plan was enacted. Rather than exact war reparations from humbled enemies, the winners actually spent considerable funds in rebuilding their conquered foe. It was a high water mark for human reaction to conflict. **Perhaps we will never again see it's equal.** *However, it is quite important to note that, in a continent which had known thousands of years of fighting, intra European warfare is unthinkable today. Just four days before the Sandy Hook shooting, the Nobel committee awarded the European Union with the Nobel Peace Prize, pointing to the reconciliation between Germany and France after the Second World War as the beginning of 60 years of European peace.*

*   *   *

Churchill and Roosevelt redeemed us all by being magnanimous in victory and setting the stage for lasting peace. Accommodation and compromise at its finest.

And yet, having now made the case **for** compromise and the rebuilding from ruins after a tragedy, let us present an opposing cautionary tale. It is also one of high compromise, intended to build a nation, but instead left 200 years of human suffering as its legacy. And I fear it is more applicable to our current circumstance.

Anecdote 13: Slavery; our peculiar institution

At the time of the Constitutional Convention in Philadelphia in 1787, twenty five of the Convention's fifty five delegates owned slaves, including all of the delegates from Virginia and South Carolina. It was a big problem facing the delegates who had a nation to build, a method of proportional representation to consider, new territories to define as to slave or free, and the protection of business interests since some of the wealthiest persons of the day were in the room. This was essentially a North/South issue, since slavery had virtually disappeared in New England and yet was perceived as fundamental to the then largely agricultural economy of the South. This division threatened the very Union itself, as some southern states threatened not to join the new constitutional government without slavery being protected. Compromise, negotiation, tabling to committee and all the intrigue and baroque techniques of parliamentary procedure were employed. In the end, to allow compromise, much of the subject – including Congress' ability to ban the international slave trade - was tabled for 20 years. Did this help? No. It just kicked the can down the road, with enormous and painful costs in human suffering.

Time and time again, the subject came up, because of its injustice and because the new territories forced the issue. New England was the large financier of new territories, but the slave owners were often the ones who wanted to develop the open and arable land.

*The Fugitive Slave Law of 1850, and all the debate and legal fights that led up to it, forced the North to face up to their implicit support of slavery. **This was a revolution where the people were at odds with their legislatures.** While the Federal Government and several states were making compromise, citizens like Harriet Beecher Stowe, who wrote Uncle Tom's Cabin, were marshalling public support against the Fugitive Slave Law and slavery in general. It was an impossible situation to find compromise.*

Even when war started in 1861, Washington was want to avoid making any decision on slavery. Maj. Gen. Benjamin Franklin Butler was on the front lines in charge of Fort Monroe, VA. As Lincoln said to General Butler, "the business you are sent upon . . . is war, not emancipation". Butler was in a unique position of holding a fort in the middle of recently declared hostile territory. In the spring and summer of 1861, slaves began escaping to his fort for liberation and protection on a daily basis. Butler had a decision to make. All this political compromise was at odds with growing public sentiment. Fort Monroe was largely manned by New Englanders, who were clearly abolitionists. Yet in his inaugural address, President Abraham Lincoln said. "I have no purpose, directly or indirectly, to interfere with the institution of slavery in the states where it exists," the President said. "I believe I have no lawful right to do so, and I have no inclination to do so."

So as with so many decisions, it was up to the people to take matters into their own hands and fight what they saw was an unjust set of laws. Butler, a lawyer in civilian life, decided he had the authority to hold them. As the <u>NY Times</u> said, "if the Southerners insisted on treating blacks as property, this Yankee lawyer would treat them as property, too. Legally speaking, he had as much justification to confiscate (the escaped slaves) as to intercept a shipment of muskets or swords. "

Butler knew ending slavery was the fundamental question of this conflict. "Shall we now end the war and not eradicate the cause?" the general wrote a friend that summer. "Will not God demand this of us now he has taken away all excuse for not pursuing the right?"

Long before Lincoln and his cabinet would make their own decision regarding slavery, citizens and this one citizen officer led the cause with resolute purpose. As a result of this fight, a change in mind set evolved throughout the whole nation. As the NY Times said in an April 2011 article, "Just as influential was what did not happen: the terrible moment — long feared among whites — when slaves would rise up and slaughter their masters. It soon became apparent from the behavior of the contrabands that the vast majority of slaves did not want vengeance: they simply wanted to be free and to enjoy the same rights and opportunities as other Americans. Many were even ready to share in the hardships and dangers of the war. Millions of white Americans realized they did not actually have to fear a bloodbath if the slaves

*were suddenly set free. This awareness in itself was a
revolution. "*

*   *   *

We know the fight for equal rights for black Americans did
not stop in 1865. Even after emancipation, it would take a
hundred more years, employing marches, boycotts, sit-ins,
riots and non-violent civil disobedience, before anything like
equality was guaranteed to black citizens. The point here is,
reform came from below and flowed upwards, not top down.
This change, long in coming and painfully won, was made by
citizens first, determined to fight a government not acting in
either their own interests or the interests of a group that
could not defend itself. Unlike the case of the Atlantic
Charter and the Marshall Plan, abolition and civil rights did
not come from statecraft but rather from civilian activism.

And that brings us to our present issue - the case of gun
ownership in America and its overt public health threat to our
emotionally distressed citizens and to our youth. Do we
follow the WWII model and wait for statesmen like Churchill,
Roosevelt and Marshall to emerge? Or do we follow the
abolitionist/civil rights model and take on this task as a
people. Judging from the stalemate in Washington
regarding the debt crisis and Congress' inability to even pass
an assault weapons ban, the path is clear; we have no
statesmen, so the people must take it upon themselves to
effect change.

The three pivotal groups who tipped the scales in the last
election were women, African Americans and Latinos. And
these are the very same groups who need to mobilize and
become vocal if real change in our gun culture is to ever take
place. The very groups most likely to perceive gun
ownership as a threat are the very groups that are in the
ascendancy and only need to own their new status in order
to use it. The example of the New York legislature acting so
fast was solely due to a clear message from the electorate.
Politicians will respond if the people speak with a loud and

clear voice. But the task is ours to initiate. Waiting for politicians to take the lead is a futile dream.

But how bold should this initiative be? Can this "minority majority" be as magnanimous in victory as the allies were after WWII? Hopefully so. Yet is compromise (or some middle ground) even possible? How can one compromise with the lives of our youth?

Furthermore, can an exit strategy be found for a shrinking yet entrenched and fearful subset of our society? Gun owners seem to possess a wide variety of fears. Efforts to change their mindset seem to only inflame those fears even further. It is a complex educational challenge that will not be easy resolved. Yet we ignore this situation at our peril. The violence implicit in a small, heavily armed and angry minority would be a threat to all of us.

*   *   *

"By folly & misconduct (proceeding from a variety of causes) we may now & then get bewildered; but I hope, and trust, that there is good sense and virtue enough left to bring us back into the right way before we shall be entirely lost."
George Washington

Section Three: Conclusions and Recommendations

Some but not all of the conclusions and recommendations in this section already exist in previous chapters. They are repeated and summarized here for convenience. Where appropriate, chapter numbers are shown in parentheses for further reference.

The overarching conclusion of this study is that gun availability poses a threat to almost everyone (Ch. 10). At the worst moment in someone's life, when they are making the most terrible decision they've ever made, a gun will greatly increase the likelihood of a fatal outcome. Whether their intention is to commit suicide or homicide, the mere presence of a gun elevates an event from a momentary and fixable error in judgment into a permanent and unfixable tragedy (Ch. 1, 8).

We know all humans make bad choices (Ch. 7). Regardless of all the other steps we can take to mitigate those bad decisions, a certain number of bad human choices will still remain. When those bad moments occur, we can only hope there isn't a gun at hand to make things worse.

Consequences from homicides and suicides affect all of our society, not just the victims (Ch. 9). With so many of our citizens at risk and with the enormous costs, social and financial, caused by every homicide and suicide, this isn't someone else's problem. It's everyone's problem. Therefore, gun owners and their lobbyists must own up to the very idea that this is a public health issue, not a rights issue (Ch. 2).

The protection and improvement of community health is the primary role of our public health authorities. In providing that role, it is appropriate that our government promotes the practice of public health by encouraging us to avoid dangerous activity. These circumstances are no different than their telling us to reduce texting while driving or warning citizens about the twin dangers of inactivity and obesity. If we are to reduce the enormous number of firearm deaths each year, we need to teach an entire nation the basic principle; that these guns increase risk, not reduce it (Ch. 12).

Surprisingly, this perception of risk is not universally accepted (Ch. 12). We have learned that the prevailing attitude of most gun buyers – both legal and illegal – is that guns will bring them an increase in personal safety. And yet the evidence found in highly credible research points overwhelmingly to the reverse conclusion; that in fact, the presence of a gun actually increases danger to its owner rather than reduces it. This represents an enormous failure of perception and in order to reverse this we need a national educational program. And as a public health issue, this education effort should be publicly funded. There are existing models available to follow, such as the one we used to teach that smoking causes cancer (remember how the tobacco industry fought that one).

There are many barriers to our understanding which will make this education program more complex than previous public health initiatives (Section Two). At the heart of this misperception about safety are some deeply seated fears resulting from demographic changes in the makeup of America (Ch. 14,15,16). Intercultural understanding and humanizing "the other" will greatly reduce fears and should consequently reduce gun purchases.

It's going to take a rigorous public debate and carefully considered thinking as to how we can make our country open and safe for everyone. There are many legislative and social policy steps we can take right now which would have immediate impact. With so many lives at-risk, waiting is not an option. The pages that follow contain specific policy recommendations. The list is by no means exhaustive but it represents a start. And start we must. No threat to American lives is greater.

20.

Summary of Legislative Policy Proposals

The unmonitored and uncontrolled private markets are the principal source for weapons used in crimes (Ch. 4). These markets might include many guns that started their existence in a legal transaction, fully registered with background checks, and used by a law abiding citizen. But they didn't necessarily end there. These unregulated secondary markets make getting a gun too easy. And it is that easy availability that puts us most at-risk.

Therefore, it is urgent that we extend the current regulations for purchasing a gun from its present limitation of just gun dealers to the additional markets of private sales and gun shows (Ch. 4). Secondly, we must improve the quality of background checks by greatly expanding state reporting to the National Instant Criminal Background Check System (NICS). All the best legislative policy proposals out there include these two overarching principles.

As a consequence, I support Americans for Responsible Solutions, former Congresswoman Gabby Giffords' group, which promotes an enhanced system of background checks, making that requirement universal including private sales. Further, I support adding the Terrorist Watch List to the list of people prohibited to purchase guns. All these steps would prevent more criminals from buying guns.

New York's Senator Charles Schumer proposed a bill, *S. 436 (112th): Fix Gun Checks Act of 2011*, which would have made good progress on improving the background check system by increasing reporting from the states on criminals, the seriously mentally ill, and other prohibited purchasers to the National Instant Criminal Background Check System (NICS). That bill died, but we need another like it.

Another model bill came from Senator Kirsten Gillibrand, *S.2878 (111th): Gun Trafficking Prevention Act of 2009* which tried to help law enforcement prevent gun trafficking. Since guns used in crimes throughout the US come from only a few dealers in a few states, tracing data and anti trafficking laws are urgently needed.

It is long overdue that we repeal the Tiahrt Amendments which unreasonably restrict the ability of law enforcement, state and local government officials, Members of Congress, and the public to access valuable data on traced crime guns (Ch. 4,12). We need to do this to promote research which can better inform our decision making. It is ridiculous to be facing such a major public health care risk while wearing a self imposed blindfold.

After a remarkably unified message from the electorate, the normally ineffective New York State legislature rapidly passed the Secure Ammunition and Firearms Enforcement Act of 2013 (NY SAFE ACT), which is designed to keep guns out of the hands of potentially dangerous mental health patients and ban high capacity magazines and assault weapons (Ch. 15). In part, it does this by requiring complete reporting by local mental health officials and a new registration database. It also requires tracking of high-volume ammunition purchases in real time and eliminates online internet purchases of ammunition. And it closes the private sale loophole. It is a model for all other states to follow.

I look for the repeal of any state laws designed to restore firearms rights to those who lost them for mental health reasons, and a repeal of *S.669 (111th) Veterans 2nd Amendment Protection Act*, since procedures for assessing if someone is no longer a threat to public safety are ill-defined and vague and the courts who administer it are not equipped to make a mental health assessment.

Clearly there should be a limit on the capacity of magazines as there is no good reason anyone would need these except to commit mass murder (Ch. 13).

I look to the NRA, supported by a national buyback program, to help address the issue of legacy guns (Ch. 5). Since guns outlive their owners and all the control at point of purchase and all the banning of new guns will never make the old one's go away, we need a plan to address the hundreds of millions of weapons which will change hands in the next 30 years, to make sure they don't fall into dubious hands long after a law abiding owner lost control of them through age, illness or death. The very existence of these legacy weapons can represent a permanent threat to future generations, probably not because of the original purchaser, but because of a distraught family member or less than law abiding heir.

As the world's number one weapons dealer, it would be profoundly disingenuous of the US to worry about firearm deaths in our own country without considering the consequences of American made products killing people in other countries (CH. 6). As the biggest player in this market, we must support and pass the UN's Arms Trade Treaty being voted on later this month.

21.

Summary of Social Policy Proposals

Our most at-risk citizens are our youth and those emotionally prone to commit suicide (Ch. 2, 8). These are the two groups most likely to die from a firearm injury. There are a variety of social solutions that can make a real difference with both groups. The overarching principles to good social policy include;

> 1)   A national education program, based on successful strategies from other public health initiatives such as car safety or youth tobacco prevention campaigns, to help the public be better informed so that their decisions regarding guns are in their best interest (Ch. 2,18,19).
> 2)   Collaboration with local community leaders, educators, police and district attorneys and religious leaders in a comprehensive approach of job opportunity, non violence coaching, educational encouragement, intervention to prevent or suppress gang activity, and concerted efforts to keep firearms out of the hands of our youth (Ch. 2). The goals are to change community norms and perceptions of new alternatives to gangs and violence.

The best broad based community programs seem to be the ones utilizing the CeaseFire Chicago and Save Our Streets models (Ch. 2). As with so many others, I support expansion of these programs to all major cities. In fact, 100% of the author's proceeds from this book are being donated to CeaseFire. Money spent on these programs prior to a life of crime will be far cheaper than money spent afterwards on policing, judicial process and incarceration.

To help prevent gang membership in the first place, we need more after school programs and work programs to give our youth a place to be besides the street and a more optimistic view of their economic future by giving them an entry point into a life of productive work (Ch. 2). Programs that need to be studied, promoted and replicated include New York State's Youth Works Program which encourages businesses to hire unemployed and disadvantaged youth ages 15 to 24, and New York City's many afterschool services which support young people and working families. Many of these programs suffer from a lack of funding in the current economic climate and yet investment up front in our youth will reduce crime, increase the number of productive members in our society and save us money on the back end in less judicial and incarceration costs. Detailed analysis of several working programs can be found in a 2010 Rand Corporation Study entitled *Hours of Opportunity: Lessons from Five Cities on Building Systems to Improve After-School, Summer, and Other Out-of-School-Time Programs.*

Social policy which reduces suicide is not as easily defined as those which reduce homicide (Ch. 8). Besides reducing the availability of a firearm at one's most vulnerable moment, the additional solutions to preventing suicides seem complex and not easily summarized or fully known. However, we do know they will involve education in both causes and identification of persons most at-risk, along with efforts to reduce the stigma associated with getting care, plus increased access to mental health care and additional research both in the nature of suicides and the accumulation of best practices as various groups work to solve this national health crisis. A useful study entitled *Charting the Future of Suicide Prevention: A 2010 Progress Review of the National Strategy and Recommendations for the Decade Ahead* prepared by the Suicide Prevention Resource Center (SPRC), is worth reading for its prescriptive value.

Looking at

22.

Last Thoughts

Whatever policies and programs we enact, it will be the citizens who lead this effort, not our political leaders in Washington (Ch. 19). Judging from the stalemate regarding the debt crisis and Congress' inability to even pass an assault weapons ban, the path is clear; we have too few statesmen, so the people must take it upon themselves to effect change.

The three pivotal groups who tipped the scales in the last election were women, African Americans and Latinos (Ch. 16). And these are the very same groups who need to mobilize and become vocal if real change in our gun culture is to ever take place. The very groups most likely to perceive gun ownership as a threat are the very groups that are in the ascendancy and only need to use their new status. Politicians will respond if the people speak with a loud and clear voice. But the task is ours to initiate. Waiting for politicians to take the lead is a futile dream.

Appendix: Reference sources

ABC, "Hate Groups Grow as Racial Tipping Point Changes Demographics", Colleen Curry, May 2012

Anderson, Terry, and P. J. Hill. *An American Experiment in Anarcho-capitalism: The Not So Wild, Wild West,* 1979.

American Public Health Associations, *Investigating the Link Between Gun Possession and Gun Assault,* 2009

Bloomberg Businessweek, "Guns Don't Kill People, Gun Culture Does", Charles Kenny, January 2013

Bodge, George Madison, *Soldiers in King Philip's war,* 1896

The Boston Globe, "The gun toll we're ignoring: suicide", Leon Neyfakh, January 2013

Bradford, William, *Of Plymouth Plantation,* 1651

Center for Court Innovation, *Testing a Public Health Approach to Gun Violence," An Evaluation of Crown Heights Save Our Streets, a Replication of the Cure Violence Model,* Sarah Picard-Fritsche and Lenore Cerniglia, 2012

Center for Disease Control and Prevention (CDC), *Leading Causes of Death by Age Group, Black Males-United States,* 2006.

Center for Disease Control and Prevention (CDC), *National Center for Injury Prevention and Control, Nonfatal and Fatal Firearm-Related Injuries,* 2001 to 2010

Center for Disease Control and Prevention (CDC), *National Vital Statistics Reports,* October 2012

Congressional Research Service, *Gun Control Legislation,* William J. Krouse, November 2012

CNN, "Gun rights groups say Georgia home invasion proves their point", Rich Phillips, January 2013

CNN, "Newtown opens eyes to other gun violence against young people", Sarah Hoye, January 2013

Current Biology, *Intergroup Empathy: How Does Race Affect Empathic Neural Responses?*, Joan Y. Chiao , Vani A. Mathur, June 2012

Department of Justice, *Best Practices To Address Community Gang Problems*, October 2010

Emerson, William K., *Marksmanship in the U.S. Army: A History of Medals, Shooting Programs, and Training*, May 2004

Federal Bureau of Investigation, *Crime in the US Study*, 2010

Federal Bureau of Investigation, *National Gang Threat Assessment – Emerging Trends*, 2011

Firearm & Injury Center at Penn, Firearm Injury In The U.S., February 2011

The Gallup Organization, *Annual Crime Poll*, 2005

Gottfredson Associates, *Gang Problems and Gang Programs in a National Sample of Schools*, 2011

The Guardian, "Shakespeare is still relevant in schools", Jacqui O'Hanlon, November 2009

The Guardian, "West overlooked risk of Libya weapons reaching Mali, says expert " Ian Black, January 2013

Harvard University School of Public Health, Harvard Injury Control Research Center, *Homicide*

The Hill, "UN votes to reopen talks on arms-trade treaty opposed by NRA", Jonathan Easley, December 2012

The Hill, "Waxman urges attention to mental health in gun debate", Elise Viebeck, January 2013

IBISWorld Report, Tank *and Armored Vehicle Manufacturing in the US*, October 2012

John Hopkins School of Public Health, "Study Finds Federal Amendments Increased Gun Sales Diverted to Criminals", January 2012

Jones, James Rees, *The Anglo-Dutch wars of the seventeenth century*, Longman, 1996

Journal of Quantitative Criminology, *The Monetary Value of Saving a High-Risk Youth*, Mark A. Cohen, 1998

The JRank Psychology Encyclopedia, *Suicide/Suicidal Behavior*

King, Jr., Martin Luther, "A Time to Break Silence," speech delivered in NY on April 4, 1967

Life Magazine, "Faces of the American Dead in Vietnam: One Week's Toll", June 1969

Mother Jones, "A Guide to Mass Shootings in America", Follman, et al., February 2013

National Institute of Health, *The Cost of Crime to Society: New Crime-Specific Estimates for Policy and Program Evaluation*, McCollister et al., April 2010

National Opinion Research Center (NORC) at the University of Chicago, *General Social Survey (GSS)*, 2012

New England Journal of Medicine, "Guns and Suicide in the United States", Miller et al., September 2008

New York Times, "How Slavery Really Ended in America", Adam Goodheart, April 2011

New York Times, "Guns and Suicide", Jeffrey Freedman, February 2013

New York Times, "Rift With Buddhists Seems to Widen in Vietnam", David Halberstam, June 1963

New York Times, "Share of Homes With Guns Shows 4-Decade Decline", Sabrina Tavernise and Robert Gebeloff, March 2013

New York Times, "Some With Histories of Mental Illness Petition to Get Their Gun Rights Back", Michael Luo, July 2011

New York Times, "To Reduce Suicide Rates, New Focus Turns to Guns", Sabrina Tavernise, February 2013

New York Times, "To Stem Juvenile Robberies, Police Trail Youths Before the Crime", March 2013

Office of Juvenile Justice and Delinquency Prevention , *The National Juvenile Justice Action Plan*, 1997

The Pew Charitable Trusts, *Collateral Costs: Incarceration's Effect on Economic Mobility*, 2010.

Pierce College, *Gangs: A Criminological Issue*, October 2012

The Rand Corporation, *Hidden in Plain Sight; What Cost-of-Crime Research Can Tell Us About Investing in Police*, Paul Heaton, 2010

The Rand Corporation, *Hours of Opportunity: Lessons from Five Cities on Building Systems to Improve After-School, Summer, and Other Out-of-School-Time Programs*, Susan J. Bodilly, Jennifer Sloan McCombs et al., 2010

San Francisco Chronicle, "Tough solutions for high school truancy rate", August, 2010

Southern Policy Law Center (SPLC), *The Year in Hate and Extremism*, Mark Potok, Spring 2013

Statesman.com, "Friendships forged around the gun at women's pistol club", Esther Robards-Forbes, February 2013

Stewart, David O. *The Summer of 1787. New York:* Simon & Schuster, 2007

Suicide.org, "Suicide Statistics", 2005

Suicide Prevention Resource Center (SPRC), *Charting the Future of Suicide Prevention: A 2010 Progress Review of the*

National Strategy and Recommendations for the Decade Ahead, August 2010

United Nations, *The arms trade treaty,* 2013

U.S. Department of Justice Bureau of Alcohol, Tobacco, Firearms and Explosives (ATF), "Firearms Commerce in the United States Annual Statistical Update 2012"

U.S. Department of Justice, Comparing the Criminal Behavior of Youth Gangs and At-Risk Youths. C. Ronald Huff, October 1998

U.S. Department of Justice, Federal Criminal Case Processing Statistics, 1998-2010

U.S. Department of Justice, National Institute of Justice Research in Brief, Guns in America: National Survey on Private Ownership and Use of Firearms, Philip J. Cook & Jens Ludwig , May 1997

U.S. Department of Justice, Survey of State Prison Inmates, 1997

U.S. Supreme Court, *District of Columbia v. Heller,* 554 U.S. 570, 2008

USA Today, "In Guam, gun tourism is big business", Eric Talmadge, Associated Press. February 2013

University of Stanford, *Tobler's Law, Urbanization, and Electoral Bias,* Jowei Chen, Jonathan Rodden, 2009

University of Victoria, *An encoding advantage for own-race versus other-race faces,* Walker & Tanaka, 2003

Vaughan, Alden T., *New England Frontier, 3rd edition: Puritans and Indians 1620-1675,* April 1995

The Washington Post, "Industry pressure hides gun traces, protects dealers from public scrutiny", James V. Grimaldi and Sari Horwitz, October 2010

www.ingramcontent.com/pod-product-compliance
Lightning Source LLC
Chambersburg PA
CBHW060501280326
41933CB00014B/2820